Zina, Transnational Feminism, and the Moral Regulation of Pakistani Women

Shahnaz Khan

Zina, Transnational Feminism, and the Moral Regulation of Pakistani Women

UBCPress · Vancouver · Toronto

15 14 13 12 11 10 09 08 07 06 5 4 3 2 1

Printed in Canada on acid-free paper.

Library and Archives Canada Cataloguing in Publication

Khan, Shahnaz
Zina, transnational feminism, and the moral regulation of Pakistani women / Shahnaz Khan.

Includes bibliographical references and index.
ISBN-13: 978-0-7748-1285-6
ISBN-10: 0-7748-1285-0

1. Sex discrimination against women – Pakistan. 2. Women – Legal status, laws, etc. (Islamic law). 3. Women – Pakistan – Social conditions. I. Title.

HQ1745.5.K46 2006 305.42'095491 C2006-900077-8

Canada

UBC Press gratefully acknowledges the financial support for our publishing program of the Government of Canada through the Book Publishing Industry Development Program (BPIDP), and of the Canada Council for the Arts, and the British Columbia Arts Council.

This book has been published with the help of a grant from the Canadian Federation for the Humanities and Social Sciences, through the Aid to Scholarly Publications Programme, using funds provided by the Social Sciences and Humanities Research Council of Canada.

Printed and bound in Canada by Friesens
Set in Stone by Artegraphica Design Co. Ltd.
Copy editor: Robert Lewis
Proofreader: Jennifer Croll
Indexer: Adrian Mather

UBC Press
The University of British Columbia
2029 West Mall
Vancouver, BC V6T 1Z2
604-822-5959 / Fax: 604-822-6083
www.ubcpress.ca

Contents

Important Dates

1947	British India is divided into India and Pakistan.
1948	Mohammad Ali Jinnah, the founder of Pakistan, dies.
1951	Liaquat Ali Khan, first prime minister of Pakistan, is assassinated.
1958-69	First martial law regime of General Mohammad Ayub Khan.
1969-71	Second martial law regime of General Yahya Khan.
1977-88	Third martial law regime of General Zia-ul-Haq.
1979	General Zia embarks on a process of Islamization; the Zina Ordinance is part of this process.
1999-present	Fourth martial law regime of General Pervez Musharraf.

Acknowledgments

My analysis has benefited from conversations with Guida Man, Nandi Bhattia, Amina Jamal, Nancy Cook, Rhoda Howard-Hassmann, Rod Michalko, Tanya Titchkosky, Maureen Moynagh, Lavia Stan, David Lyons, Zia Awan, Lala Rukh Khan, and Cynthia Wright. Moreover, my scholarship has been strengthened by the love and support of my family, including Zainab, Raza, and Patrick.

This study was funded by grants from the Social Sciences and Humanities Research Council of Canada and St. Francis Xavier University.

This discussion draws from and elaborates on analysis that I put forward in earlier work:

"Zina and the Moral Regulation of Pakistani Women," *Feminist Review* 75 (2003): 75-94.

"Locating a Feminist Voice," *Feminist Studies* 30, 3 (2004): 660-85.

"Re-configuring Native in the Global Age," *Signs: Journal of Women in Culture and Society* 30, 4: 2017-35.

Acronyms

AI	Amnesty International
BBC	British Broadcasting Corporation
CIA	Central Intelligence Agency
CIW	Commission of Inquiry on the Status of Women
HRCP	Human Rights Commission of Pakistan
HRW	Human Rights Watch
UNDP	United Nations Development Program
USDS	United States Department of State

Zina, Transnational Feminism, and the Moral Regulation of Pakistani Women

Introduction

A short time ago, I attended a lecture by Noam Chomsky at which he spoke out against the racism faced by Arabs and muslims.[1] As part of his presentation, Chomsky pointed out that Pakistan, from which I immigrated to Canada many years ago, has the freest press in Asia. After the lecture, I got a ride home with a colleague who, like myself, teaches at an Ontario university. During our return, it became apparent that Chomsky's comments had been lost on my colleague, for he proceeded to inform me that I was fortunate to be living in Canada, where I can read whatever I like and where I am not forced to veil. He then went on to recommend that I educate myself about how muslim women are treated, suggesting the writings of Bangladeshi writer Taslima Nasrin as the best place to start. That I am a muslim and also have some first-hand knowledge of this matter didn't occur to him.

Nasrin is best known for her book *Lajja,* which examines the plight of a hindu family in Bangladesh in the wake of communal violence against hindus in Dhaka. This violence, Nasrin is quick to point out, was directly connected to the 1992 destruction of the Babri mosque in India. Despite Nasrin's attempts to challenge communal violence, Habiba Zaman (1999) notes that her work has been used by the state as well as by fundamentalist forces in both India and Bangladesh in ways that contribute to communal divisiveness. At the same time, Zaman argues, Nasrin is seen in the West as the sole feminist voice in Bangladesh who speaks out against women's oppression and against fundamentalism. What is dismissed in this scenario is the active women's movement in Bangladesh, a movement of which Nasrin has never been a part. Her story floats without a context and, as Shamsul Alam's (1998) analysis suggests, needs to be situated as occurring in an environment that is not only suffering the effects of neocolonialism and capitalism, but also facing the global trend of rising fundamentalism. However, Nasrin's decontextualized writing, like forced veiling, has become a battering ram for those unwilling to be more informed on the issues.

My colleague directed me to Nasrin's work as a way to become more informed about my own life as an unveiled muslim woman in Canada. To him and to others like him, I say: the veil was never an issue for me when I lived in Pakistan. It became an issue when I moved to Canada, particularly so when I was and am confronted with views like his. Furthermore, I have never had limits placed on my reading, in Pakistan or in Canada. I could not tell him so on that particularly cold and wintry night: I was afraid of the violence in his voice. His comments suggest an overt paternalism that also exists in a more latent form in other more "polite" remarks directed at me, such as, "a muslim woman teaching women's studies, wow, that is a first" or "a muslim feminist, isn't that an oxymoron?" These remarks attribute my agency to my living in the West and suggest that I should be properly grateful. Such comments remind me that I live in a context where the binary between Islam and the West has vigorously reasserted itself. Racism against muslims and Arabs often goes unchallenged. Instead, representations of muslims and Arabs as barbaric and cruel to women are common knowledge and used to justify war.

The recent bombing of Afghanistan by American-led forces provides an example. Statements by politicians that Afghan women need to be saved preceded American military action. Popular images of, as well as commentary on, veiled and confined Afghan women helped to construct a justification for the invasion of the country. The invasion of Afghanistan did indeed help to dislodge the oppressive Taliban regime from power; however, the situation of Afghan women is still bleak. True, the veil is no longer mandatory, but there is little employment, and violence on the street has increased since Taliban times. I fear that my examination of *zina* might similarly be used to build consensus for a military campaign against Pakistan. Not that I believe George W. Bush, or any other US president, will mount a military campaign to liberate Pakistani women. But if the world's only superpower decides that it is timely or opportune to bomb Pakistan, the plight of Pakistani women will help to convince American voters that these women need to be liberated from which ever regime is in power at the time.

Narratives of the imprisoned Pakistani women interviewed for this study might be used to confirm the position of third-world women and muslim women as victims in popular articulations. Stereotypes in everyday conversations, on television, and in films perpetuate fear and elicit laughter, more so since 11 September 2001. Stereotypes also help to sustain policies through which muslim and Arab men are identified as the uncivilized other and routinely rounded up and detained for suspicion of terrorist activity. They do not need to be charged or brought before the court. Their wives, mothers, and daughters are left to secure their release. The Mahar Arar case speaks to such a process at work in both Canada and the United States. Arar, a Canadian citizen, was deported to Syria, from where he had immigrated to Canada in 1988 at the age of seventeen. Popular reports suggest that both the American and Canadian intelligence agencies collaborated in his removal to Syria, where he was confined and tortured over a period of one year. Only through the relentless efforts of his wife, Monia Magizh, was Arar able to return to Canada. A public inquiry is underway at the time of this writing to look into the matter.

During my 1998 research trip to Pakistan, I was warned about the ramifications of the textual and visual accounts that my findings might produce. Neelam Hussain (1998), the coordinator of the women's activist group Simorgh commented:

> I am very aware that what I say against the Hadood and other laws can be twisted by western representations. CNN and Sixty-Minutes have been in touch with us at Simorgh that they want to come and look at zina and will we help them ... So one is caught ... here is another opportunity to create pressure on the government but we don't want to perpetuate more stereotypes. So at this point I am [left] thinking: Does [*sic*] the Hadood Ordinances provide another reason [for Westerners] to bomb us out of existence and into obedience? It is infuriating.

And I was also warned by Rehana Yasmin (1998), the female superintendent of Kot Lakpat prison in Lahore, who was present throughout the interviews that I conducted with the women incarcerated there under the Zina Ordinance (also referred to as the zina laws). Yasmin was concerned that I will use the women's stories to write something that would defame Pakistan to the outside world. Yasmin's point is well taken. I, too, am wary about how my findings will be read.

How then do I speak about the Zina Ordinance within such a context, an ordinance through which over one million zina cases were filed with the police and 300,00 heard by the courts during the period 1979-95 (USDS 2000, 10). This astounding statistic is made doubly sinister by the fact that the women are largely innocent and locked up on trumped up charges. How do I know that they are innocent? I know because their acquittal rate is 95 percent. The victims, who range in age from children as young as twelve years to elderly women, can spend up to five years in jail before they are acquitted and released. Many of these women are illiterate and do not know under what law they have been charged. These are the "lucky" victims of the Zina Ordinance. I say "lucky" because as impoverished women, they are able to find sanctuary in the prison from the wrath of their families and former husbands. I interviewed such women for this study.

While the Zina Ordinance has the potential to affect all women in Pakistan, this investigation does not examine how more affluent women are affected or how they comply with and resist family wishes. It is generally assumed that they are vulnerable to honour killings, which are illegal but nevertheless practised in Pakistan. Indeed, one such woman was killed recently in her lawyer's chambers when she came out of hiding to meet with her mother (AI 2002), who had brought with her the thug who gunned her daughter down and had helped to orchestrate her daughter's murder. The perspectives of the men incarcerated due to zina will also likely be of great significance to understanding how women charged with zina bargain with patriarchy. However, such an examination is also not the subject of this investigation but remains an important area of research for future studies.

Many of these middle-class women under threat of zina charges are seeking refuge in the West, and I have found myself positioned as the expert witness in some of their asylum cases. Several women have benefited from my testimony and have indeed been granted asylum. The limited format of the affidavits that I have to write on their behalf, however, makes it almost impossible to produce a historically grounded account of the Zina Ordinance and its effects. Instead, there is a risk that my affidavits will sensationalize the lives of women in Pakistan as oppressed by Islam. It is extremely difficult to produce these documents. I know that immigration judges will read them, and I know that my work will help to further their bias against other muslims, particularly men, seeking asylum or visas.

Stereotypes and the discursive strategies that such practices sustain coexist along with possibilities for different kinds of conversations that move us beyond the binary thinking of savage muslims versus civilized Westerners. Instead, we can begin to speak about how our lives are intertwined and hybrid in the diasporic space of North America. It is also a time when the antiglobalization movements allow for a multiplicity of alliances between members of diverse groups – for example, the environmental movement, human rights groups, organized labour, the gay and lesbian rights movement, and of course, the women's movement.

These alliances allow various regional and national groups to march in transnational solidarity toward a more just society.

Through such a paradigm, the local and global remain linked discursively. As I examine the local milieu, which produced and continues to sustain the Zina Ordinance, I also connect it to a larger international frame within which Pakistani patriarchies function. I am also interested in how the local and global interact to produce the conditions that women both resist and comply with in Pakistan. However, I am not content with these linkages; I push this analysis over yet another boundary. I want to remind women in the West that what happens in Pakistan is connected to how their own concerns are increasingly being marginalized. And I argue that racist determinations of women *over there* as distinct from what happens *over here* will keep interlinked global issues separate and thus work against transnational feminist solidarity. To minimize against this atomization, I look beyond connecting the local and the global and ask additional questions in this investigation: How are investigations of events connected to their representation and their reading? How can my own location as native informant help to produce a critical analysis not only for a first-world audience, but also for a third-world one?[2] As we move forward into the twenty-first century, I believe that these are crucial questions for building and sustaining feminist solidarity.

It is within such conversations that I wish to locate my analysis of the Zina Ordinance and its effects. At this point, I turn to explaining what the Zina Ordinance is and discuss its legal implications.

The Zina Ordinance

The Pakistani Constitutions of 1962 and 1973 called for the appointment of a Council of Islamic Ideology to bring existing laws into conformity with Islam. The military regime of General Zia-ul-Haq (1977-88) took this mandate more seriously than had any of his predecessors (Carroll 1982) and, in 1979, promulgated the Hadood Ordinances as a first step toward the process of Islamization. The Hadood Ordinances include the Zina Ordinance, the law governing theft, consumption of alcohol, and Qazaf (giving false testimony) (HRCP 1997; Jahangir and Jilani 1988). The Zina Ordinance censures "illicit sex" and prescribes predetermined punishment for the offenders based on particular readings of *sura* (chapter) 24, verse 2, of the Qur'an: "The woman and the man. Guilty of fornication. Flog each of them. With a hundred stripes" (Ali 1938). Conventional scholarship on legal understandings of the Sunna (the body of traditional Islamic law) interpreted this verse to mean that the punishment of one hundred stripes was to be applied only to those persons who were *not* married. For married persons guilty of fornication, the traditional view was that they should be stoned to death.

Even though prior penal laws gave secondary status to women, these laws offered them some protection (Sardar Ali 2000). Previously, adultery had come under the purview of the Pakistani Penal Code, which allowed a husband to revoke a complaint against his wife at any time. Very few cases of adultery were recorded before 1979. This changed with the promulgation of the Hadood Ordinances. The number of incidents has reached the hundreds of thousands, and the ordinances have become a tool in the hands of those who wish to exploit women (CIW 1997).

With the proclamation of the Zina Ordinance, for the first time in Pakistan's history, fornication and adultery became a crime against the state as opposed to individual husbands, fathers, or other men. Both fornication and adultery became noncompoundable, nonbailable, and punishable by death (HRW 1992, 34). A noncompoundable offence is one that the police or government may continue to investigate and prosecute even if the original complainant withdraws his or her statement implicating the accused. Individuals prosecuted on nonbailable charges are not eligible for the right of release pending trial by posting bond. Bail is left to the discretion of the judge.

Moreover, the term "zina" conflates two practices: adultery among the married and fornication among the unmarried. At the same time, the legal definition of zina blurs the lines between adultery, fornication, and rape. For the purpose of the ordinance, there is a further distinction. "Zina" is defined as sexual intercourse without being validly married, while *"zina-bil-jaber,"* rape, is defined as sexual intercourse without being validly married when it occurs without consent. Legally, this means that if it cannot be proved that sex occurred without consent (rape), then the act of sex itself becomes a crime against the state (Jilani 1998). Although the structure of the laws and the nature of evidence required to establish guilt make the lesser punishment of *tazir* (see below) more likely, if a defendant is convicted, *hadd* (or the maximum sentence) is mandatory. A person's sentence varies according to the religion and marital status of both the accused and the witness as well as the evidence on which the conviction rests (Jahangir and Jilani 1988). In the case of fornication and adultery, provided that the accused is a muslim, if (1) he or she confesses, (2) there are four adult, "pious," male, muslim witnesses to the act of sexual penetration (four female witnesses' testimony will not suffice for hadd punishment), and (3) the accused is married, then he or she *must* be sentenced to death by stoning. If a nonmuslim or unmarried accused (1) confesses and (2) the crime is witnessed as described above, then the accused must be sentenced to one hundred lashes with a whip. The maximum hadd punishment for fornication, adultery, or rape is identical (except in the case cited above as [3]). Although hadd punishments have been imposed, none have been carried out to date.

If the evidence falls short of what is required for maximum punishment, but the case is still proven, then the accused is charged under a lesser class of punishment, known as tazir. Here, unlike in the case of hadd, women may testify on their own behalf if the judge should so allow it. The tazir punishment for adultery or fornication is up to ten years in prison, thirty lashes with a whip, and a fine of an indeterminate amount. The tazir punishment for rape is up to twenty-five years in prison and thirty lashes. The terms of punishment are left to the discretion of the judge. For the purposes of tazir, no distinction is made between a married and unmarried offender. Insufficient evidence to impose a hadd punishment may still result in conviction under tazir. That is, when women are unable to prove rape under hadd or even tazir, they can be charged with illicit sex under tazir.

With the hadood laws, rape is now subsumed under the category zina, so if coercion cannot be proved, the victim becomes an offender who has enjoyed illicit sexual activity. At the same time, the rape victim has no right to testify on her own behalf. Because the Pakistani state has faced national and international pressure regarding hadd punishment, no woman convicted under these laws has been stoned to death. However, women are frequently found guilty of the lesser offence of tazir and prescribed public whippings as punishment, according to human rights lawyers and activists Asma Jahangir and Hina Jilani (1988).

The Zina Ordinance is a contested issue in Pakistan. Indeed, stoning to death for married persons as hadd punishment was challenged as early as 1981.[3] Carroll (1982) notes that in a four-to-one decision, the Federal Shariat Court (the special court where hadood and other religious cases are heard) held that the Sunna cannot alter the clear wording of the Qur'an, which calls for one hundred stripes as punishment for zina. Thus, in the opinion of the court, the maximum punishment for married as well as unmarried offenders ought to be one hundred stripes. "The Ordinance, [to] the extent that it imposed the death penalty for *[z]ina*, was thus held repugnant to the injunctions of Islam" (Carroll 1982, 72). Pressure from those who disagreed with this decision no doubt influenced General Zia, for he altered the composition of the

Federal Shariat Court within weeks of the decision and added three *ulema* (religious scholars) in an attempt to tip the balance for a more conservative reading of the law.

What is the basis of the Zina Ordinance? Is it religion, culture, or politics? Katherine Ewing (1988) identifies a tension between the codes of behaviour derived from Islam and those influenced by other sources, such as local traditions. I argue that the Zina Ordinance is located within this tension. The ordinance is against not only the Constitution of Pakistan, but also, as many have argued, the spirit of Islam. At the same time, the Zina Ordinance does provide more powerful members of families with a mechanism to control and intimidate others, especially women, resulting in incarceration for those who rebel against family wishes. In so doing, it creates new traditions capable of generating income for impoverished families and of cementing alliances by means of marriages between interested parties. Through the practices associated with zina charges, a potentially lucrative but exploitative economics gets transferred into symbolic idioms of sexuality and morality. For many women, zina is operationalized in ways that connect the process of intimidation and incarceration to monetary exchanges, highlighting the material predicaments of their families and suggesting that their economic situation is driving them to take recourse to repressive zina laws. Moreover, it leads us to speculate that control of morality and sexuality through zina might be used as a façade for material sustenance through new forms of income-generating schemes for many impoverished families, as many women's narratives suggest later on in this discussion.

The Zina Ordinance was promulgated as a means to ensure a "moral" and just society in Pakistan. However, the definition of "morality" in the zina laws is ambiguous, and the state's control over its citizens is not absolute. Thus both the reading of the law and its effects are uneven in that they are mitigated by class and gender. Women's narratives reveal that they are jailed for all kinds of "offences" that have little connection to illicit sex. Many of the women charged with zina, as I will demonstrate, have not even been accused of fornication or adultery. Indeed, many of them have been identified as accomplices to runaways. Others cite poverty, family violence, and police corruption for their plight. Impoverished and illiterate women who are unaware of the process of law and/or unable to mount a legal defence are particularly affected.

Their accounts suggest that poverty provokes many parents to marry off their daughters in exchange for money. Moreover, their stories identify deeper issues, such as corruption, poverty, drug abuse, alcohol abuse, and male violence, and point to the women's commodification by more powerful members of their families. They point to factors that place women, especially poor women, at risk. Their stories identify a society where police corruption and violence go unpunished, male violence against women has little legal sanction, and the majority of the population is increasingly impoverished. Moreover, the legal system is so backlogged that often an incarcerated person awaiting trial is held for a period longer than the sentence that he or she would receive if convicted (USDS 2000, 20). Incarceration for zina is a form of disciplinary power that Michel Foucault (1979) reminds us helps to create docile bodies. My investigation suggests that in Pakistan, women's families and the state collude in this process.

In this discussion, I argue that zina laws evoke a desire for moral purity in a context of societal corruption. They examine and identify an embodied morality that focuses on illicit sexuality. Crucially, notions of embodied purity and the absence of illicit sex render invisible the societal impurity of the nation. This impurity comes out of the economic and political corruption of the state. However, the moral regulation of impoverished women through zina laws rhetorically cleanses the symbolic impurity of the country. Although recent court proceedings have largely ruled in favour of the zina victims, these decisions reinforce class and gender relations. Women who are incarcerated in prison or more informally in the *darul amans* (women's shelters) cannot claim constitutional rights of liberty, equality, and citizenship. They are granted these rights through the judicial process, which is dominated largely by middle- and upper-class males.[4]

Although the ordinance allows families to draw on the power of the state to help regulate the sexuality of their women, this discussion will suggest that the women are not helpless victims. Instead, they often negotiate these spaces with tremendous courage and tenacity. While women charged by their families for adultery and fornication are indeed incarcerated by the state, the places of incarceration and refuge (in state-sponsored shelters) also become "safe" spaces for women fleeing the wrath of their families.

Perhaps Deniz Kandiyoti's (1991) comments about what she calls "classical patriarchy" might help us to understand how women and some men challenge injustice in China, the Middle East, India, and Pakistan. These challenges reveal a variety of ways that they accommodate and acquiesce to as well as contest and renegotiate community and familial rules. Kandiyoti notes that classical patriarchy is based on male authority backed by a material base. Women will be protected if they adhere to the feminine ideals of submissiveness and docility. This myth is under siege. Increasing immiseration of families under globalization appears to shake a similar base in Pakistan. As women's contribution to the family economy becomes increasingly essential, there is potential for them to renegotiate their status within the family and to have a greater say in family affairs. The threat of zina charges works to neutralize women's voice in the family and renders questioning patriarchal authority a very dangerous enterprise. My data suggest that in the contradictory space of prisons and the state-sponsored shelters, women are able to pose stronger challenges to familial authority and to make more effective bargains with patriarchy.

Despite a general lack of awareness about the ordinance, the narratives of the women whom I interviewed are a testimony to their endurance in the face of tremendous odds. Their narratives suggest that they know that Islam allows them to choose their own marriage partners. Yet, paradoxically, they are also socialized to accept familial authority over their choices. They attempt to reconcile these tensions by maintaining their faith in Islam. Still, women reject the interpretation of Islam that subjects them to abuse at the hands of their families and brings them into contact with a corrupt and inefficient criminal justice system. The process politicizes many of the women, and they question the fundamental principles of their socialization, particularly obedience to their families. The incarcerated women frequently desire greater independence from their families and express a need for self-sufficiency. Indeed, many take advantage of the educational and skill-development programs available to them in prison.

General Zia, the military dictator who promulgated the Zina Ordinance, expressed a desire to streamline access to the law. He believed that the judiciary and its bureaucracy did not provide cheap and speedy justice to the average Pakistani ("Editorial," *Dawn Overseas Weekly* 1978). He promised to appoint learned, pious, and muslim men to deal with cases arising out of the Hadood Ordinances. However, as narratives of the women interviewed for this study indicate, his policies made the situation worse for impoverished women. Moreover, Zia's understanding of *sharia* (Islamic religious law) suggests a one-dimensional perception of the legal process on which it is based and gestures to a larger problem, as I argue later on in this discussion, of undemocratic regimes using Islam to back up their power base. When questioned about how differing interpretations of Islam would be handled within his Islamization program, Zia replied, "We are not getting into that debate. We are going to the basic laws. *Qur'an* and *Sunnah*. We are not going into various schools of thought" ("Editorial," *Dawn Overseas Weekly*

1978). By focusing on the "fundamentals" of Islam, Zia's vision denied not only the complexities of Islamic traditions, but also the complexities of the Pakistani context, with its deep cleavages based on gender, class, and religion.

Paradoxically, people in the Canadian context also often focus on the fundamentals of Islam and reproduce decontextualized accounts of muslim women and other third-world women, which my colleague so forcefully projected onto me. His comments remind me of my political quandary. I have found that speaking about the injustices that women suffer because of the Zina Ordinance is an interesting exercise in Pakistan. Many of the activists and jurists whom I have met are against the laws, and they, too, speak out against the suffering that the laws are causing. At the same time, young Pakistani women are getting messages from films and advertisements that create and reinforce symbols and metaphors of both the good and bad woman. The former, through her docility and chastity, is able to escape male violence, while the latter, who actually acts on her desire, is not (Sher 1996). Furthermore, popular accounts of zina victims in local tabloids suggest that they are loose women with suspect morals who deserve to be charged and incarcerated for not having the requisite feminine attributes of docility and obedience.

Speaking in Canada is another matter. Here I find myself confronted with the popular perception that all muslim women are oppressed by Islam. I am in a bind. On the one hand, speaking out against the injustice of the Zina Ordinance is important. At the same time, I fear that my critique of the conditions in Pakistan risks reinforcing dominant stereotypes about third-world women and muslim women.

Chapter 1 examines this quandary. I locate myself as a native informant who is producing knowledge about Pakistani women for a Western audience. I argue for a feminist analysis that reflects on the practices of textual production and that requires the researcher to be responsive to issues arising both from her location and from the location of the people whom she is researching.

Earlier in this Introduction, I described the legal implications of the Zina Ordinance. However, if the ordinance remains decontextualized, my account threatens to reinforce stereotypes of muslims and third-world peoples as barbaric and uncivilized, similar to the stereotypes that have accompanied conventional readings of many writings by Taslima Nasrin. In Chapter 2, therefore, I turn my attention to providing a context for the Zina Ordinance. I investigate the historical association of religion with the forces of power in Pakistan and also with the international powerbrokers in the region. I argue that religion remains connected to nationalism in Pakistan and that politicians have used these linkages for short-term gain.

Chapter 3 examines the spaces and conditions of women incarcerated for zina. I also identify the circumstances under which I was given access to women in prison and in the state-sponsored women's shelter, or *darul aman*, at Lahore.

In Chapter 4, I argue that the majority of the women have been sent to jail by their families for not obeying family wishes. Yet the women's narratives suggest that they are not helpless victims of their relatives. Instead, the process of incarceration politicizes many of the women, and they frequently use their spaces of confinement to upgrade their literacy and income-generating skills as they equip themselves to negotiate better bargains with patriarchy.

Chapter 5 examines how the feminist women's movement consolidated to challenge the antiwoman aspects of Zia's Islamization. I identify the current conditions that continue to sustain the antiwoman laws in Pakistan. I argue that, in view of the corruption of the state, introducing morality has become a major issue for Pakistani politicians. The state, however, has little power to regulate the moral behaviour of any but the most vulnerable citizens – illiterate and impoverished women – through its regimes of discipline. These women suffer the most under the zina laws.

Chapter 6 challenges liberal feminist voices that promote a cultural-relativist position of examining the third-world woman *over there*. Instead, through a reconfigured native informing, I aim to identify and work toward the destruction of the power relations that sustain native informing. Such a process connects conversations about the woman *over there* to the woman *over here*. In so doing, I (re)locate the zina laws as an issue not only for the third world, but also for transnational feminism.

1
Native Informing on the Zina Ordinance

Locating the Problem

In a recent article entitled "'Under Western Eyes' Revisited: Feminist Solidarity through Anticapitalist Struggles," Chandra Mohanty (2003b) revisits her earlier critique (1991) of liberal feminism and its tendency to produce sensational accounts about third-world women as the oppressed other. Mohanty once again argues for a reading of women's oppression in ways that show the local and global not only as simultaneous, but also as constitutive of each other. Mohanty's analysis contributes to an examination of my location as a native who informs on the Zina Ordinance for a Western audience. In so doing, I reconfigure conversations about the native so that she is positioned to inform not only on the Zina Ordinance in Pakistan but also on its reading in the West.

The Zina Ordinance is an extremely oppressive, controversial, and contested piece of legislation in Pakistan. I am able to voice my criticism to Pakistani government officials who frequently agree with me and to activists there who are working to secure the release of women imprisoned for zina. Most people I have spoken to agree that, no matter how many safeguards the *ulema* (religious leaders) have put in place to mitigate the consequences of false accusations, the effects of the Zina Ordinance on the lives of its victims are devastating. Moreover, the hundreds of thousands of cases to which it gives rise use up scarce resources in the incarceration of under-trial prisoners, an incarceration that can sometimes be as long as several years. At the same time, Pakistan's overloaded justice system is further backlogged. These are general issues that many human rights lawyers, jurists, feminists, and other progressive people discuss with each other in Pakistan. I, too, have been a part of these conversations.

Voicing my criticisms of the Zina Ordinance in Canada is another matter. Speaking of its excesses and wanting to bring about social change situates me and other Pakistani women who live in the West in a theoretical and political double bind. As Marie-Aimée Helie-Lucas (1999, 278) suggests in another context, we are silenced by the fear of being accused of betrayal by members of our own communities. Here I specifically refer to the diasporic communities in the West, where idealized notions of home circulate freely. And we are also aware that criticism of third-world cultures often serves to further demonize and stereotype third-world peoples, reinforcing a view that seeks to free brown women from brown men (Spivak 1989). Yet, after hearing the voices of the incarcerated women, I must speak. I do not, however, want to present a decontextualized account of the Zina Ordinance. Drawing on the notion of the native informant, I want to explore how geography, politics, and racialized culture help to shape the debate on the zina laws in Pakistan and their reading in the West. Speaking about the Zina Ordinance in the West positions me as a native informant, a person who informs or explains the rituals or traditions of her people for the researcher, the explorer, the outsider. It is a process, Trinh Min-ha (1989, 59) reminds us, through which the natives, as subjects of research, are "the handicapped who cannot represent themselves and have to either be represented or learn how to represent themselves."

An unproblematic use of this role in the process of knowledge production has been critiqued in recent years (e.g., Narayan 1997; Spivak 1995; Visweswaran 1994). Akhil Gupta and James Ferguson (1997, 37) have called for a continued rethinking and revitalization of anthropological fieldwork so that we move toward "a sense of a mode of study that cares about, and pays attention to, the interlocking of multiple social-political sites and locations." Gupta and Ferguson further suggest that we identify and examine places, peoples, and predicaments through more dynamic ethnographical studies that are able to take advantage of the opportunities generated by such flexibility. The predicament of the third-world researcher living and working in the first-world yet whose field of research is a third-world site provides an example of a study with creative and dynamic potential.

With more researchers from other parts of the world living in and writing from Western diasporic locations, the one who researches *over there* may not be white or male. She may be, like myself, a racialized woman who is not seen as part of the first world despite living and working there. Thus she is not only on the perimeters of a male academy, but also on the fringes of liberal feminism. Perhaps she is an ex-colonial critical of continued colonialism in its new forms. Marta Savigliano (1995, 11) has noted that colonial discourse works to keep such an insubordinate ex-colonial in her place. My analysis challenges this process, as it extends the idea of the "field" so that it includes not only the site *over there,* where I search for answers to research questions, but also a second site *over here,* where my research will be read.

Traditionally, comments by native informants have reinforced stereotypes of the third-world woman and the muslim woman. I am interested in conversations that help to reconfigure the native informant's role by making visible and challenging the power relations that sustain it. I particularly want to challenge the notion of neutral knowledge and help to generate some accountability in the process of writing and its reading.

Challenging Neutrality

In recent years, social theorists Trinh Min-ha (1989), Gayatri Spivak (1999), and Uma Narayan (1997) have begun to shake the ground of neutrality and argue that knowledge is socially produced through a process in which the producer and reader are thoroughly implicated. Drawing on these arguments, I grapple with the following questions in this discussion: How does my location both in Canada and in Pakistan help to determine the type of work that I do with women in Pakistan? To what extent do I help to reinforce stereotypes about the Pakistani, the muslim, and the third-world woman? Am I forever doomed to strengthen racism when I challenge the sexism of antiwoman laws in Pakistan? How might I mitigate these effects?

Such questions allow me to move beyond relativist perspectives that present ahistorical accounts or problematic cultural and religious explanations for events. They facilitate debates that provide context by identifying the social and political circumstances surrounding the issues. Of particular significance is an examination of re-presentation and editing practices through which events are retold as they travel from the third-world to the first. Homi Bhabha (1994a) reminds us, however, that the context does not travel as well as the stereotypes do that sustain sensational stories. I also question why certain issues such as female genital mutilation and forced veiling cross over readily, while others like malnutrition and lack of clean water and housing do not. A conventional examination of zina laws would suggest regulation of the Pakistani female's sexuality, evoking images of the other woman caught in illicit sex and jailed by her fundamentalist culture. Testimonies of women suffering under zina laws might reinforce both variants of Orientalism:[1] denied and available sexuality. Accounts of how the Hadood Ordinances and, in particular, the zina laws have impacted Pakistani women's lives have tremendous potential to become yet another sensationalized third-world women's issue.

My project challenges liberal frameworks that, Spivak (1999, 352) claims, enable the native informant to present true accounts from a position of fixed identity. Such problematic frameworks would perhaps generate desire among some to liberate Pakistani women from the oppressive forces of Islam and local patriarchs. In her article "Do Muslim Women Need Saving," Lila Abu Loughad (2002) examines such paternalism and maternalism. Although I challenge similar sentiments directed toward Pakistani women, I do not want to deny that Pakistani culture includes state-sanctioned laws that help families to socially and sexually control "their" women. I do, however, argue for a contested notion of culture as a more appropriate view within which to understand the Zina Ordinance. In so doing, I complicate notions of identity and culture based on Orientalist stereotypes that result in simplistic descriptions of muslims and, in this case, Pakistanis. Moreover, I recommend an integration of *here* and *there* and reidentify intertwined histories of home and location, origin and diaspora, that complicate the production and reception of knowledge. Such analysis, and accompanying strategies of action, might examine the role of national and global struggles in defining and constituting the "sacred" in Pakistan.

Reading the Zina Ordinance in the West

My concerns about how my research on the Zina Ordinance might be received in Canada are well illustrated through a British Broadcasting Corporation (BBC) documentary entitled "Murder in Purdah," which aired on the Canadian Broadcasting Corporation (CBC) in January 1999 on the *National Magazine*. The opening segment begins with the words "Women are jailed on the rumour of adultery in Pakistan and men kill their wives to protect their honour." Moreover, commentator Brian Stewart warns us that some of the scenes we are about to see may be disturbing. The text goes on to inform us that "Riffat and Ahson marry without parental permission and Karachi exploded." The juxtaposition of text and images is dominated by a narrative of the rise in Islamic fundamentalism and connected to eruptions of violence. Scenes depict terrifying images of armed male Pakistanis rioting in the streets, burning, shooting, and looting. None of this mayhem in Karachi is shown to be related to further devaluation of the rupee and the resulting rise in food and fuel prices or to the lack of employment opportunities, growing poverty, and degradation connected to globalization. Neither is the massive influx of arms from Afghanistan given any mention. There is no evidence of investigative reporting on the easy availability of firearms, a legacy of the Afghan war, in which the Pakistani government under General Zia-ul-Haq, with financial and moral encouragement from the United States and Saudi Arabia, aided and abetted the Afghan rebels.

Instead, the presentation suggests that the people of Karachi, the financial capital of Pakistan and a major seaport on international trade routes, have nothing better to do than worry about who marries whom. Moreover, the only hope of survival that Riffat and Ahson have is to find asylum in the West. In simplistic terms, the couple are seen as victims of their society, culture, and religion whose salvation lies in escape to the West. The scenario of West as best and West as the place of civilization where all must go to be saved has repeated itself once again. Yet another scenario has repeated itself as well. In her analysis of the politics of imperial wars and benevolent interventions, Sedef Arat-Koc (2002) suggests that people who were interested in saving Afghan women from the Taliban are usually critical of feminist concerns in their own country. There is nothing new in this situation. Eugene Cromer, the head of the British colonial administration in Egypt from 1885 to 1907, had similar sentiments. On the one hand, as Leila Ahmed noted (1992) he wanted to save Egyptian women from Egyptian men; on the other hand, he was one of the founding members of the antisuffragette movement in England.

Conventional visual and textual imagery on the third-world woman suggests that the Eastern woman is a victim and that the Western woman is liberated. Such comparisons minimize and make more difficult critiques of violence and other structural inequalities that women face under Western patriarchies. These views also help to mystify and disarm women in North America and Europe by pointing out that their lot is better than that of those *over there*. How, then, do I proceed? And what are the implications of performing a critique of the zina laws for a largely white audience?

A descriptive presentation of the zina victims might recall Stanlie James' (1998) warning about the invisibility of progressive struggles in popular Western conceptions about the third world while provoking strong reactions similar to those evoked by the practices of *sati* and female genital mutilation.[2] Victims of zina laws might become the new hot topic, generating countless student assignments and magazine articles and perhaps providing, as did accounts of the victims of Taliban atrocities, the impetus for consciousness raising about the issues. Such consciousness raising is important not only for generating awareness, but also as a tool for pressuring local and international powerbrokers. Yet it is not without a price. My staging of Pakistani culture will likely support Eurocentric views of the other as barbaric and, as Coco Fusco (1998, 367) has pointed out in another context, confirm popular racial stereotypes while building support for repressive domestic and foreign policies. Clearly, practices through which particular subjects inform on the natives are harmful and must be situated as arising out of unequal social and political relations. It is to this process that I now turn.

Locating the Native Informant

It would seem that writing about the repressive zina laws is an easy thing to do. But it is not so simple. As a "third-world" feminist and a postcolonial subject, I am ambivalently positioned within an identity that invites me to speak both as the victim and as a subject who, as Uma Narayan (1997, 3) points out, "often feels forced to give an account of itself." Literary, cultural, and political pressures position me as a unitary subject, a third-world native informant (re)producing the voice of alterity. Situated in the West and producing accounts of zina laws through the voice of the other woman, I am damned if I do and damned if I don't. For, as Trinh Min-ha (1989, 80) comments, "You try to and keep on trying to unsay it, for if you don't, they will not fail to fill in the blanks on your behalf, and you will be said." As a native informant, I realize my no-win situation, and I am silenced. I struggle to recover my voice and wonder if I can do ethical research. Daphne Patai (1991, 150) reminds us, however, that "in an unethical world we cannot do truly ethical research." I accept Patai's statement.

But there is more. The first and third worlds are discursive and material divisions based on power and wealth. The disparities that accompany these divisions place me, a person who lives in Canada and does research in Pakistan, in a contradictory position. These contradictions arise partly because of the inequalities between *here* (the first world) and *there* (the third world), but also because I (a middle-class academic) am researching "down" by focusing on impoverished and imprisoned women. Given that the contradictions cannot be resolved, at least in the foreseeable future, I strive for transparency and reflexivity in the process of research itself.[3] Moreover, I turn my attention away from trying to resolve the contradictions and toward furthering the discussion of the native informant. I focus instead on repositioning, refiguring, and reconceptualizing conversations about the role of the native informant.[4] In making these connections, I recover my voice. But first I must disrupt the conflation of the other woman *over there* and the one who speaks for her *here*. Although the two women are situated differently, they have intertwined histories. Interrogating these histories allows us to understand how the production of knowledge is related to its reception and how my account of the zina laws and their effects is connected to my ambivalent positioning within the academy.

The Native Informant *Over Here*

The forces of neocolonialism and globalization have helped to trigger economic, ecological, and military disasters. Many people, particularly from the third world, have been displaced because of these conditions. Millions of refugees, immigrants, temporary workers, and "illegal immigrants" or undocumented workers have come to the first world as part of the diasporic gatherings of people in North America and Europe. I, too, have come to the so called new world to find justice and economic welfare in a capitalist society. And I find that, as a third-world feminist, I am positioned as the native informant within the academy. A native informant, as Spivak (1999) reminds us, identifies the struggle between identity and difference (both *over there* and *here*), as she is situated to present a totalizing account of her nation and her community. She is the authentic insider who, Narayan (1997) points out, is recruited into a role where she is pressured to perform her authenticity. Notions of what is authentic do not allow for creative and independent thought and action but channel us to conform in particular ways and are extremely oppressive.

In the imagination of the nation that I call home, Canada, I, too, am present only at the fringes and discover, as Spivak (1999, 398) suggests, that white capitalist culture accepts native informants to the extent that we "museumize" or exoticize our national origin. At the same time, powerful texts of the master discourse appropriate my voice, while stereotypical images of muslim women suggest fixed static identities. Stereotypes are, as Homi Bhabha (1990, 70-1) reminds us, the fixed static constructions of the other, which, although already known, are constantly repeated. These repetitions include the usual commentary about the third-world woman as passive, emotional, oppressed, victimized, and subservient to her men. In the case of muslim women, the list also suggests that she is veiled, exotic, and oppressed by Islam (Alloula 1986; L. Ahmed 1992).

Positioned as a third-world academic, I am channelled into doing research on third-world women either in Canada or in the third world whether I want to or not. Coded as a third-world woman, I frequently face unwritten expectations that I will research topics that deal with third-world women's issues. Comments made by a journalist who had investigated a variety of topics both in Pakistan and in the Middle East support my position. She indicated that in Canada she was considered competent to write only about issues dealing with third-world women or muslim women. Disillusioned by this process, she has given up journalism. I, too, believe that my choice of research topic stems as much from external pressures as from my own interest in the topic. I am also aware that my investigation of the zina laws will likely confirm the popular myth that, as a racialized woman, I cannot and do not work on the issues of "normal" or "regular" people, who Richard Dyer (1997) reminds us are what white people often think themselves to be. Racialized people are expected to take up the issues of race because it is considered their issue. Well-meaning, progressive white academics, on the other hand, will routinely ignore the fact that they, too, are racialized (as white), commenting that they are not familiar with race literature or that it is not a field that they have chosen to examine. Yet, is not understanding difference and its effects a shared responsibility?

My body bears the markers of race and gender; as a result, I am considered the "expert" in this area. This categorization accompanies an expectation that a large segment of my course curricula will be on race and gender. Often racialized women find that only they are teaching these issues, a situation that has repercussions. As bell hooks (1994) reminds us, studies in race and gender often entail a considerable amount of unlearning that is painful and that at times produces a reaction among students. This reaction, with its accompanying anger, is often projected onto racialized women by otherwise well-meaning students. Performing the native can be a stressful rite.

A related aspect of the stereotypical categorization concerns the determinants of the types of work that I do. In previous research, I chose to investigate the lives of muslim women in Canada, but in a sense the work also chose me. It stemmed from my own contradictory positioning in Canada around the time of the Gulf War. I found that I had no place from which to speak that did not take me toward an Orientalist rejection of myself as muslim or an uncritical embrace of religion. My subsequent research and analysis contributed to an understanding that women's lives cannot be constrained within predetermined boundaries.[5] Instead, I drew on women's narratives to examine the in-between hybrid lives within diasporic space in the West. Similarly, my work on imprisoned women in Pakistan, although informed by a desire to help bring about changes, is also to some extent an artefact of my contradictory positioning in Canada. Both my projects – my examinations of muslim women's lives in Canada and of women's experiences of the Zina Ordinance – are investigations of women's narratives. As I bring their voices into the larger conversation about women's issues, I am particularly interested in identifying how my respondents deal with the complexities of their lives.

Although I speak of identity as complex, contested, and socially determined, in Canada my work risks being co-opted by ethnic studies or multicultural studies. Such programs often define the research and scholarly activities of myself and other women of colour through which we perform our versions of authenticity and difference. Although these spaces do provide us with anchors to our identity and at times access to funds allocated for minority studies, they are also problematic. With its emphasis on examinations of events within predetermined cultural and national borders, ethnic studies exacerbate binaries that reinforce views of Orientalism and as two sides of the same coin (Chow 1997, 6). Such a process not only reduces third world societies into denigrated and exotic others but also identifies each difference in authentic terms; animalistic Africans provides an example while terrorist muslims provides another. At the same time it discourages an examination of the West and East as interconnected in favour of an examination of the two as ontological absolutes. Within this paradigm, performing a critique of the Zina Ordinance and speaking of its excesses would constitute a first-class sensational spectacle commanding attention as I, the authentic feminist voice of Pakistan generate a text that appears to condemn all Pakistanis, muslims, and other such people. Or even worse, Pakistani women's struggles might be further co-opted and appropriated within liberal discourse so that we become, as Trinh Min-ha (1989, 82) reminds us, someone's private zoo. The depoliticization that accompanies such ghettoization and appropriation allows for, as critical theorists have pointed out (e.g., Rattansi 1992; Gilroy 1987), a containment of ethnicity that does not provide space for examining what is at stake in terms of local and international contestations and hierarchies.

Gayatri Spivak's comments support these views. She argues that the native informant's voice is often appropriated, rendering her complicit in knowledge production about the third-world other. Living in a diasporic space in the West, my voice, too, risks being appropriated, and I likewise become complicit in producing knowledge about the muslim. My complicity shatters any attempts to evoke "true" knowledge. Within such a location, Spivak does not recommend that I attempt to produce true accounts. Instead, she argues, the native informant should remain a reminder of alterity. As I struggle toward a strategically effective method of looking at the complexities and contestations of speaking to the excesses of the zina laws, I realize that no matter how I present the situation, to a certain extent my account will reinforce the view of Pakistan and the third world as a violent and uncivilized place for a substantial portion of the readers. I accept this as a limitation of my work.

There is yet another aspect of native informing. While my colleagues in Canada expect me to do research on Pakistani or other third-world women, in Pakistan I was considered not Pakistani enough. Gayatri Spivak (1995, 149) has written about this "continuous testing of the expatriate by the locals." While on recent research trips to Pakistan, I was welcomed as a Pakistani. But local activists also continuously reminded me that I was not one of them: "For an outsider you seem to know quite a bit about what is going on here," one Pakistani journalist commented after she had read my work. Others argued that I was not a stakeholder in negotiating the issues in the same sense that they were, as I did not share their risks. I was positioned differently. Some remarked, "You will go back to your academy and write your research and we will have to continue to deal with the Hadood and other repressive laws," while others commented that "After all, this law does not really affect you; you are an outsider, you come and go." These comments led me to ask myself whether I was somehow seen as a traitor or unworthy because I had left.

How then do I respond to the idea that I may not be authentic enough to be taken seriously by Pakistani activists and feminists? It is true that I am located differently from Pakistani activists. I am not subject to the coercive power of the state in the same way that they are, although, as a former Pakistani national and now a visitor to Pakistan, I am subject to all Pakistani laws, including the zina laws, while in the country. I can, however, unlike activists in Pakistan, return to my home and my academic position in Canada. It is likely that Pakistani feminists are leery about committing energy to relationships with researchers who, they say, "come and go." After an absence of over thirty years, I am new to the Pakistani scene. Nevertheless, my continued commitment to the issues in Pakistan will, I believe, help me to build solidarity with local feminists.

Feminist discourse, however, both *here* and *there* is marginal to mainstream debates. I am an outsider to marginalized feminist debates in Canada because I am not white and, in Pakistan, because I do not live there. Situated as an other of the other, I am reminded that the position of native informant has to be continuously negotiated. The native informant is an authority on third-world women. Yet, as Spivak (1999) has argued, I, too, believe that the authority of my claims is continuously deferred to the Western academy for legitimization, identifying once again my complicity in reproducing the master narrative about third-world people. This concern is echoed in the continuing challenges that I face by the locals in Pakistan whose comments indicate that I am not one of them and have been somehow tainted by years of living in the West. Such views suggest that my research is not relevant to Pakistani struggles.

Although some feminists and activists in Pakistan may determine that my work there is inconsequential, I do not accept that my work is irrelevant. As a feminist committed to change, I believe that patriarchy in the West helps to prop up patriarchy in the third world, including Pakistan. As feminists come together in international collaborative projects, they can identify the ways that patriarchy and capitalism work across national borders. Through this understanding, we can imagine and forge more internationally based resistance.[6]

In a sense, the woman-of-colour native informant is positioned within academia with a preset script. She performs the other, the model member of her group, and does not upset the status quo. Such a process suggests an appropriation of her body and voice. Within academia, the native informant has become commodified, her body and voice bought and sold. Upon hiring her, in a sense the university "buys" representations of the person, rendering her ethical position for sale. Similarly, publishers "buy" the texts she produces, frequently to identify themselves as inclusive. Granted the academy is normally not welcoming to feminists; however, these comments are particularly valid in the case of women of colour. What kind of choice does the native informant have? If she does not perform her role or performs it in ways that suggest resistance, she will likely be censured. Chances are that no one will publish her work. What happens if she gets out of line? Likely, she will be fired or be silenced in other ways, such as through isolation and exclusion. It seems that the native informant has to behave.

Not only is the subject position of the native informant problematic, but Spivak (1989, 269) raises a cautionary voice about "making false claims to alternative histories." She suggests that we closely examine the social and historical process that has created particular people as native informants who are at once an object of analysis as well as the subject of a particular form of knowledge. Such a process conflates the indigenous elite woman in local sites with the diasporic intellectual turned native informant. Spivak reminds us that both are products of colonial and neocolonial education and complicit in the production of knowledge about the gendered subaltern whom they claim to represent.

Writing about zina places me in a complicated struggle, which Aijaz Ahmed (1992, 84) identifies as that of a particular privileged class that often has access to Western forms of education both in the metropole and in the colony. I, too, am a product of colonial education in Pakistan and of its liberal version in the West and am complicit in this process.

The Native Informant *Over There*

In my reconfiguring of the native informant, I want to recognize the third-world woman *over there* who is also so positioned. As she speaks her truth in countless oral and pictorial testimonies for Western consumption, hierarchies between the researcher (often first-world) and the researched (often third-world) are rendered invisible. Particularly relevant are Daphne Patai's (1991, 137) comments that research itself depends on a subject-object split through which the objectification of the object of research and her exploitation for the research agenda are integral to the design of the project. This danger increases, Patai warns us, "when the researcher is interviewing 'down,' that is, among those less powerful (economically, politically, socially) than the researcher herself."

While interviewing the women, I was constantly reminded of inequalities between us. There was I, employed, professional, academic, free, while they were unemployed, often illiterate, and imprisoned. Not only was the interaction asymmetrical, but I am also not sure what our conversations meant to the women. Did they willingly recite their stories to me or because the prison officials had asked them to? Did they think that I might be able to help them to get released from prison? Frequently, they had anecdotes that they wanted me to include in my writing. "I am against judges, write about that please," one woman commented. Did they think that the report (as they called it) that I was writing would help to change their circumstances? Or did they speak to me because they had found someone who appeared sympathetic and was willing to listen to their narratives of sorrow and resistance? Was their encounter with me merely a diversion from the routine of prison life? Walking away from the prison to write my "report" in the form of another academic paper for which I would receive professional recognition, I was uneasy. Our interactions did not appear to translate into a tangible and immediate benefit for them.

There is another aspect to native informing. Conventional accounts present a view of the woman *over there* as monolithic. Such views also render invisible indigenous hierarchies and contestations. For example, the third-world woman is largely presented as oppressed and voiceless, leaving those activists who are struggling for human rights and women's rights largely invisible (James 1998; Mani 1990). In Pakistan impoverished women face zina charges and imprisonment. Middle-class women activists as well as others who are trying to secure their release are confronted with the sexism and corruption of government officials. They also have to deal with being labelled "Westernized" partly in response to the foreign funding that their nongovernmental organizations (NGOs) receive. But there is another reason as well. The NGOs frequently identify themselves as "secular," a designation that puts them at odds with the increasingly fundamentalist rhetoric of the state. As the weak Pakistani state moves toward closer alignment with fundamentalist forces, many secular activists have commented to me that the space for their social and political action feels increasingly narrow. Indeed, many claim that they are able to negotiate the system safely only because of their personal and family connections. Additionally, faith-based organizations and the secular NGOs frequently do not work well together. Speaking about women in domestic abuse situations, one activist working with a women's rights NGO claimed, "We do not have the same vision of women's role in the family. The faith-based organizations want family unifications at all cost, while we want to present other options to her. They want the woman to be literate in order to read the Qur'an. We want her to able to read and write and to know her rights under the law."

Moreover, the secular activists are susceptible to charges that they are Westernized and therefore irrelevant to local struggles. Attempts to dismiss feminism as a Western import have been persuasively challenged by Narayan (1997), who argues that charges of Westernization are connected to a desire to uphold the East-West binary that sustains an inability to view issues as interlinked in an international frame for resistance. Third-world feminists' concerns are generated from issues arising in their own national contexts and fuelled by a history grounded in women's resistance to subordination (Anzaldua 1987; Narayan 1997). Although these concerns are similar to those put forward in feminist agendas, it is likely that many women in the third world, as in the first, frequently see these concerns as personal and advocate change at an individual level. Feminist responses to women's subordination, on the other hand, as Narayan points out, will include analysis of women's subordination as systemic and requiring collective action. Furthermore, Narayan argues, the label "Westernized" is unevenly applied. Paradoxically, World Bank funds used to buy arms are not Western, but if funds from the same source are used to organize against antiwoman laws, the label "Western import" is often applied. "Westernized" thus becomes a label used to devalue and chastize individuals and organizations who are asking for change.

I too have been labelled "Westernized" both *there* (because I did not stay) and *here* (because I am not authentic enough). As I produce knowledge for the Western academy about the Pakistani other, I too am complicit in perpetuating the hierarchies between the researcher and researched. Yet my complicity does not come from a place of stability. Rather, I face, as Himani Bannerji (2000, 65) puts it, "the paradox of both belonging and non-belonging." To the Pakistani activist who accused me of not sharing her risk, I say, "Yes I do not face personal risks like the activists in Pakistan. I face other risks."

I do not want to suggest a hierarchy of risk, however, that seeks to determine whose risk is greater – that of the woman *over there* or that of the woman *over here*. Both have the unfortunate position of the native informant whose agency is constantly under threat. While the woman in Pakistan risks the coercive power of the state and a corrupt police force, my textualizations risk generating myriad accounts replete with oral and pictorial examples of incarcerated women. No doubt such accounts would sensationalize women's lives as once again oppressed by Islam. Through these accounts, the other issues that Pakistani women face, issues that make them more vulnerable to the zina laws, fade into the background. Indeed, as I will show in Chapter 4, sex is only one of the reasons for women's imprisonment. Moreover, sex workers do not remain in prison for long. They have the resources to secure bail. For the majority of the women in prison, poverty appears to be a much larger issue. Moreover, their poverty is connected to lack of employment, education, and housing as well as to lack of state protection against the many forms of violence that they face. In Pakistan and elsewhere, such conditions frequently accompany debt restructuring at the dictates of international agencies such as the World Bank and the International Monetary Fund.

What the Native Informs

There appears to be a visibility of native informants: they/we are everywhere speaking their/our monolithic truth, which conforms to the truth of Western Orientalism and perpetuates the dominance of Western forms of knowledge. At a gathering in the university where I taught until recently, Nepalese women spoke about poverty and violence in the lives of women in their country. Their remarks generated support and solidarity from the audience, but also promoted a cultural relativism. The violence was attributed to a problematic culture *over there*. The discussion that followed allowed Nepalese culture to be pathologized, demonized, and measured, if silently, against the "proper" treatment of women, read as Western treatment of women. What remained unexamined in the ensuing debate were the struggles that women and other activists are waging in Nepal. Also not identified was how the country's positioning within international relations of inequality helped to fuel poverty and contributed to the violence.

As native informants are invited to speak about oppressions that women face in the third world, indigenous and racialized women's concerns in the West are minimized. Moreover, people forget that women earn 70 cents to the dollar that men earn or that they come up against a glass ceiling when seeking career advancement. They do not remember that thousands of women in the first world face physical, emotional, and sexualized violence every day. Through these omissions, frequently lost is the opportunity to examine how oppression in diverse contexts is interconnected. Instead, the narratives of native informants are often given special space as the authentic voice of the violated other. Often, not individuals but spectacular stories (like female genital mutilation and the veil) are picked as representative of native informants, and then people are found whose lives are mutilated to conform to the desired spectacle. What is at stake in this process? Who gains and who loses? By drawing on the native informant's voice, the dominant groups maintain their position of privilege and label themselves the "good guys" who have benevolently given space to the native informant and have included her in their projects. This inclusion is a whitewash for the appropriation of voice and the commodification of the native informant.

Roland Barthes (1972) has spoken of the use of symbols in spectacles. Bodies and events are emptied of their history and embedded with new meaning. Barthes' comments remind me that my subject position has been slotted into Islam. As I perform the native and speak about the zina laws, I am once again inviting the viewer to the familiar view that Islam is crushing women. I am therefore suspect. I am suspect to myself: can I do ethical research? Others are also suspicious of me: is she authentic enough; will she betray us? Although the good native means a different person to each of these positions, they all want to know whether I am going to be a good girl. This is my triple bind, and I risk alienating one or all each time I speak. For me this is a politically paralyzing position. How then do I resist this subject position? How can I produce an account of the zina laws that can fuel feminist collective action? How might I write in ways that challenge Orientalism and are also responsive to local conditions? I believe that I can move out of the triple bind by initiating several conversations about native informing. One of the conversations concerns an emphasis on accountability and transparency, while yet another conversation reinforces the need for transnational feminist solidarity. Chapter 3 of this manuscript deals with the former conversation, and Chapter 6 deals with the latter. Transnational feminist solidarity links local and global practices. Such links help to determine the interconnectedness of our lives as well as the most effective kinds of action needed for change. Contextualizing the issue is an essential part of the path to transnational solidarity. It is to a discussion of the context that spawned and continues to sustain the Zina Ordinance that I now turn.

2
Contextualizing the Zina Ordinance

Locating the Zina Ordinance

The Zina Ordinance comes out of a social, historical, and political process that linked the national and political aspirations of the muslims of British India to religion. This process intensified with the call for creation of the State of Pakistan and continues to fuel diverse political agendas. Pakistani political actors, without a clear political base in terms of popularity, support, and mandate, frequently draw on religion and participate in a discourse on morals that they are not generally known to exhibit. As John Esposito (1986) notes, political regimes in power, as well as their opponents, have used Islam to legitimize themselves. Such practices have drawn on and strengthened ideas about women as markers of religious and nationalist identities. As a result, control of women's sexuality and mobility, particularly through the Zina Ordinance, has been part of the nation-building project.

Powerful visual and textual signifiers of nation and religion render ideas about zina, or illicit sex, a significant regulator of normative morality. Judgments about morality and immorality inform the state practices that women suspected of zina encounter in their dealings both with the police and with the judicial and penal systems. These judgments are used to assess and monitor actions and attitudes of the victims. As women are compelled to tell their stories during incarceration, many prison officials, as well as legal and medical personnel, claim that their accounts are lies. Yet lies and the manipulation of events might be a necessary response by women to the discourses, ideologies, institutions, prohibitions, and practices to which they have been subjected. Challenging them, these sources of coercion, means questioning not only religion, but also the symbolic force that created and sustains the State of Pakistan. I now turn to a brief analysis of how religion and nationalism have supported each other in the process of nation building.

Religion and the Nation-State of Pakistan

The Zina Ordinance emerges from a process that created and sustains the State of Pakistan. In Pakistan state and religion continue to be linked in a symbiotic embrace. The process of lobbying for, and finally securing, the State of Pakistan by the Muslim League and its leader, Mohammad Ali Jinnah, linked nationalism to religion. The country was imagined as a homeland for muslims of British India. In the subsequent process of the partition of colonial India in 1947 into India and Pakistan, over ten million people were displaced and millions murdered as they moved (both ways) across the newly created national border between the two countries. A large number of hindus moved to India, while millions of muslims fled to Pakistan. Recent literature on partition narratives (Hasan 2000) suggests that nationalism may not have been the only factor in urging people to move elsewhere. Marking particular people as members of religious communities made many unsafe in their homes and neighbourhoods and compelled them to move. Security concerns notwithstanding, nationalism continued to be important for the identity of millions of displaced persons pouring into Pakistan across the border from India, for the concept of nation, as Homi Bhabha (1994a, 139) has persuasively argued, "fills the void left in the uprooting of communities and kin." Ideas of nationalism have been pivotal in uniting the diverse people of Pakistan. At the same time, religion was also often articulated as nationalism, even as politicians expressed a desire for a secular state. This process has a particular history.

The experience of muslims under British colonial rule helped to channel visions for postcolonial Pakistan. What was referred to by the British as the Great Mutiny of 1857 was, many believe, the last stand of the muslim and hindu aristocracy against the consolidation of colonial power in India. After their defeat by the British, muslims believed that their community in particular suffered negative consequences for rebelling against the British. Some muslims began a series of accommodations with imperialist rulers that included a modernist, European-style education as promoted by Sayyid Ahmad Khan. The bureaucracy that functioned as the civil service, a major powerbroker in Pakistan, emerged from these Westernized institutions of learning. Indeed, many of Pakistan's early politicians were civil servants.

While some muslims took advantage of a Western-style education to secure employment and power as members of the bureaucracy, others refused to accommodate the colonial power. Many muslims were angered by the collapse of the Caliphate in Turkey after the First World War and joined in the Khalifat Movement hoping to reinstall the actual and symbolic supremacy of a muslim ruler as the head of an international Islamic community.[1] Seyyed Vali Raza Nasr (1994) argues that the Khalifat Movement reinforced communalism between muslims and hindus and led to greater manipulations of muslim religious symbols as a basis of group identity.

Religious symbolism, then, has been a considerable force in Pakistan, playing at least two interconnected roles in the country's early history, when it was used to foster both political agendas and Islamic revivalism. Although integrally connected to nationalism, the influence of religion has depended on the needs of the regime and the leanings of the key players within it. Moreover, religion is frequently articulated as tradition, and neither those who consider themselves secularists nor those who promote revivalism are totally free from the influences of the other. Instead, the agenda promoted by most regimes contains significant components of both. I now turn to examining how Islam was used by self-professed secularists to promote their various political agendas.

Furthering Political Agendas

Prominent political leaders who fought for the independent State of Pakistan and subsequently became its political leaders, including Mohammad Ali Jinnah and Liaquat Ali Khan of the Muslim League, called for a State of Pakistan based on a two-nation theory. Since muslims and hindus, they argued, were two nations within India, their national aspirations must have political form in an independent Indian subcontinent. Jinnah and Liaquat, along with the majority of the Muslim League, demanded a new muslim state from the British on the basis of religious differentiation. At the same time, they were calling for a secular and pluralist Pakistan. Indeed, Jinnah's vision for a muslim State of Pakistan granted full and equal citizenship for religious minorities. In his inaugural address to the Pakistan Constituent Assembly, Jinnah (1989, 46-7) stated: "We are starting with this fundamental principle that we are all citizens and equal citizens of one State ... Now I think we should keep that in front of us as our ideal so that Hindus would cease to be Hindus and Muslims would cease to be Muslims, not in the religious sense, because that is the personal faith of each individual, but in the political sense as citizens of the State."

The demand for a pluralist secular state satisfied the urban middle class, comprised of christians, hindus, and parsis. At the same time, the leaders of the Muslim League were aware that the majority of people in what would become Pakistan lived in rural areas and were under the control of the landed gentry, who use religion to supplement their own power base. Jinnah needed to please both of these major constituencies. In what appears to be an attempt to reconcile the tensions between the two, Jinnah professed both secularism and pluralism. At the same time, he manipulated religious symbolism not only to demand a new state, but also to maintain a power base in the rural areas. Faced with regional- and feudal-based divisions, Jinnah noted that a vote for the Muslim League was a vote for a state for united muslims, while a vote for the Indian National Congress meant a vote for hindu rule for an independent India. The Muslim League's famed slogan serves as an example of the link between religion and the nation-state: "Pakistan ka matlab kiya hey? La ilaha ila'llah" (What is the meaning of Pakistan? There is no God but Allah).

There is another aspect to the appeal of religion. While Pakistan is a multilingual, multicultural, and multiregional society, the army is dominated by Punjabis. Because the country has been under military dictatorship four times in its short history, prominence in the army has given Punjabis considerable political power. Mohajirs, Pathans, Baluchis, Sindhis, and at times even Punjabis have challenged government power. Faced with ethnic challenges from these regional groups, even secular modernist leaders have found it expedient to appeal to religion to develop a national unity based on Islam (Ahmed 1999). Such practices established a trend early in Pakistani political history through which Pakistani politicians drew upon religion to legitimize various agendas.

Demanding a state on the basis of religion is one thing; sharing power with religious authorities is yet another. Pakistani politicians have not wanted to share power with religious scholars, the ulema,[2] but neither have they wanted to offend them. Instead, many political leaders seem to have chosen to obscure the issue. However, the tensions between the various religious forces and secularists have haunted political leaders in Pakistan with varying degrees of intensity and have been addressed according to the social and political constraints of the times and the individual personalities of the leaders. Each political leader responded to this contradiction in a sharply different way. Many Pakistani politicians, including Zulfikar Ali Bhutto, his daughter Benazir, and Nawaz Sharif, pandered to Islamic radicals for short-term political gains. Until the current military leader, General Pervez Musharraf, decided to reign in the radical Islamic elements after the events of 11 September 2001, only one other Pakistani leader had dared to openly challenge religious authorities. He was Mohammad Ayub Khan, a military general who seized power in 1957 and held it until 1969. In his autobiography, *Friends Not*

Masters, Ayub Khan (1997, 209) identified radical Islamic leaders as "obscurantists who frustrate all progress under cover of religion." Despite Ayub's misgivings, the ruling class of this newly created State of Pakistan frequently resorted to religion to legitimize its actions; it also aligned itself with imperialist powers, particularly Britain and the United States.

I have identified several powerful players in the Pakistani political field: the landed aristocracy, the civil service, and the army. Many of these forces have recruited religion into the service of nationalism. As Shahnaz Rouse (1997) points out, once religion becomes the basis of nationalism, there is always the potential to rely on it for asserting national identity and for using it as a unifying force.

It was generally believed, Ziaul Haque (1983, 375) notes, "that the independent state of Pakistan would be a social democracy based on the egalitarian system of Islam." This system was attributed to an undefined Islamic past without any indication of how this past might provide a blueprint for a modern industrial society. As the policies and practices of Pakistan developed to benefit its imperialist allies and the local ruling classes, abstract notions of religious ideology were developed to justify state decisions, both locally and in its continued alignment with capitalist interests. This religious gloss, Haque (1983) argues, was useful to the ruling class, even as their decisions impoverished the working class.

Although the connection between religion and nation building has been present since the creation of Pakistan, it intensified during General Zia-ul-Haq's time in power (1977-88). When General Zia usurped power from the democratically elected prime minster of Pakistan, Zulfikar Ali Bhutto, in 1977, he attributed many of Pakistan's social and political problems to an "un-Islamic way of life" (Ahmed 1983). Poverty, labour strife, and rising indebtedness, in Zia's view, had little to do with internal and external structural conditions generating inequality. Instead, a lack of individual and societal morals was responsible for social woes. The solution to these ills, Zia believed, was a program of Islamization called Nizam-e-Mustapha (Governance Inspired by the Prophet). Zia's Islamization, Aijaz Ahmed argues, included a form of collective purification through the removal of impure and undesirable elements from society, either by death or imprisonment. Beginning in 1979, a series of laws and ordinances was passed to ensure that this collective purification would take place. The brutal fist of the Pakistani army, of which General Zia was chief of army staff, ensured that these new edicts were enforced.

Islamic Revivalism

Religion was also important for those muslims of the subcontinent who were interested in an Islamic revival. Mawlana Sayyid Abu'l-A'la Mawdudi founded the Jamat-i-Islami in 1941,[3] a political party devoted to the revival of a holy community based on Islamic law (Nasr 1994). Mawdudi objected to the secular leadership of the Muslim League and labelled the modernist Jinnah a *kafir*, or unbeliever. Although he anticipated Islamic revival unfolding in a united postcolonial India, Mawdudi eventually came to terms with its partition and in 1947 migrated to Pakistan, where he directed efforts to destroy the secular state and to create an Islamic theocracy. The Jamat-i-Islami was largely sidelined in Pakistani politics until General Zia's military regime assumed power in 1977.

The Zia regime provided the Jamat-i-Islami with considerable patronage, at least in the early years. Zia's interest in Islamic parties was twofold. He needed to legitimize his military coup within the country, and alliances with Islamic parties, particularly with the Jamat, seemed to provide him with this legitimacy. Additionally, Zia appeared sympathetic to the teachings of Mawlana Mawdudi and incorporated some of his demands into state ideology (Nasr 1994). For example, Mawdudi's views, with their focus on regulative and punitive aspects of religion, influenced policies and practices of the new regime.

At the same time, Mawdudi's vision for Islamization does not appear to move the state toward reducing inequalities between citizens or sharing power. Zia's vision of a model Islamic state also seemed in line with that of the Jamat, which drew support largely from the lower middle class – the petite bourgeoisie. Nasr (1994) reminds us that members of the Jamat have not appeared to be particularly interested in the plight of the poor. Instead, the Jamat agenda is more directly focused on interpreting issues through the prism of religious exegesis. Consequently, while the Jamat wins over converts to its cause, it does little to act as a political movement for social change. I found evidence of these policies in my visits to Pakistani prisons. The Jamat women run classes in the prison where they teach women how to read and interpret the Qur'an. While they appear interested in women's religious education, I found no evidence of any help provided to women in dealing with their legal difficulties or in training them in skills that would make them employable on the outside.

As part of the move toward a more theocratic State of Pakistan, its history was also rewritten. The official discourse during Zia's time denied the tensions that Jinnah had managed between the secularists (a group to which Jinnah himself belonged) and the religious orthodoxy.

Instead, Zia's regime promoted a view of Jinnah as an upholder of Islam. As a result, Pakistan's religious roots were reinforced, giving greater currency to the perception that Pakistan was created for muslims and muslims alone.

A major problem with drawing on religion as inspiration for state policy and practices is that there is no definitive Islamic text anywhere; religious rules and doctrine are deeply contested issues. In what may be an attempt to minimize challenges to a singular version of Islam, Zia's vision of Nizam-e-Mustapha was vaguely defined. Moreover, Zia's focus on Islam as his regime's source of inspiration did not prove to be a cohesive unifying force for the nation. Instead, sectarian violence increased as different groups fought to maintain the dominance of their version of Islam. Although Zia drew upon the Jamat for support, he remained firmly in control of the process of Islamization. In 1979 he stated that Islamic law would be supreme in the land. Yet, a year later, he placed himself and the military courts above the Islamic legal system (Weiss 1986a). These actions, as Anita Weiss (1986a, 12) points out, are contrary to *sharia*, which states "that the ruler must govern in consultation with his subjects and the *Sunnah* is to have final authority at all times."[4] The alliance between the Jamat and Zia was at its strongest in the period 1977-79 but failed in the long run due to the Jamat's stronger commitment to Islamization (Nasr 1994).

The arrangement with the Jamat was beneficial to Zia on at least two levels. First, it allowed the military regime to identify and neutralize the apparatus of the Pakistan People's Party, the party of the ousted prime minister, Zulfikar Ali Bhutto. Second, it helped Zia to secure a more broadly based electoral legitimacy, which his military regime did not possess (Nasr 1994; Toor 1997; Shaheed 1997b).

State patronage during the Zia regime certainly helped to institutionalize Islamic groups within the state structure, a legitimacy that they did not obtain through the political process, in which they performed dismally. During Zia's tenure, tens of thousands of Jamat-i-Islami supporters were appointed to the judiciary as well as to the civil and military service. In a sense, Zia sowed the seeds of puritanism in the army, a major powerbroker within Pakistani politics. Zia was not the first politician to encourage puritanism in the country. His predecessor, Zulfikar Ali Bhutto, who enjoyed alcohol like many members of his social circle, ironically caved in to radical Islamic pressure to ban alcohol in 1977. This ban was enforced more strictly in Zia's time, particularly in the officers' mess of the armed forces, where alcohol had previously flowed freely. Zia also encouraged the Tablighi Jamat, an Islamic organization aiming to bring spiritual awakening to muslims and which promotes jihad through conscience rather than through the sword, to become active in the army. Religion was integrated into the syllabus of all educational institutions, including the army staff college (Saigol 1994), while all Qur'anic verses pertaining to war were distributed in military circles. Religious radicalism thus continued after Zia's death because its promoters were now part of the state and the army in large numbers.[5] In effect, Islamization strengthened ties among Islam, the Pakistani state, and the military. The needs of the state and its view of Islam were backed by the muscle of the Pakistani military. At the same time, the needs of the military and its international supporters, including the United States, were to be legitimated by state interpretations of Islam.

Interrogating the Zina Ordinance

Recall that the laws and ordinances giving legal impetus to Zia's Islamization included the Hadood Ordinances, which deal with the offences of prohibition (consumption of drugs and alcohol), zina (rape, adultery, and fornication), theft, and *qazf* (perjury). The negative effects of the Zina Ordinance on women were compounded when in 1984 Zia passed the Law of Evidence. This new law reduced the weight of a woman's evidence to half that of a man; in other words, the evidence of two women would now be equivalent to that of one man. The Hadood Ordinances do not appear to be limited to purifying Pakistani society. They also seem to be timely responses to political challenges from a woman, Benazir Bhutto. Daughter of Zulfikar Ali Bhutto, she was his political heir and one of Zia's most vociferous opponents, calling for a return to democracy at the time. As these laws adversely affect women and limit their entitlement as citizens, they also ensured a debate about whether Benazir, a woman, could be head of the Pakistani state.

Moreover, as Shaheed and Mumtaz (1987) note, the Zia regime issued directives in 1982 that limited the presence of women in the public sphere, including the amount of skin that could be exposed on television and in advertisements. These directives, like others curtailing women's freedom, did not produce lasting change in Pakistani society. They were followed for a while but eventually disregarded. Despite being largely dismissed by society, these directives do, however, reinforce customary ideas about the good and moral woman who accepts the *chadar aur char divari* (the veil and the four walls), suggesting confinement and invisibility as her ideal option. The regulation of her mobility and sexuality/morality through social practice as well as through laws and ordinances remains a crucial component of the social order.

Despite Zia's attempts to curtail women's presence outside the home and to produce moral citizens, his polices and ordinances exist alongside other images of masculinity and femininity. Sadia Toor (1997) argues that the ideal male image centres on the militarized muslim male and is accompanied by escalating sexual and physical violence both in the public and the private sphere. At the same time, Pakistani women, like those in other nationalist-religious paradigms, continue to be symbolized as cultural markers within a madonna-whore dichotomy. The chaste ideal woman has minimal presence in the public sphere, where the image of the whore or tramp dominates. Even when the chaste woman is depicted, she is highly sexualized. Lala Rukh Khan (1997) directs our attention to this binary representation of sexualized women in Pakistani films and larger-than-life advertisement billboards where chaste obedient women coexist alongside tramps. These images suggest that women's power, frequently framed as sexual, is also larger than life and needs to be controlled. Indeed, control of female sexuality is a central component in strategies of socializing moral citizens. These messages are certainly present in Pakistani cinema, which, as Ferida Sher (1996) notes, largely caters to an illiterate and economically disadvantaged class. Film songs are immensely popular in Pakistan and are a very potent method of projecting messages outside the cinema halls. Sher argues that popular film songs reinforce notions of female desire as self-sacrificing and susceptible to unrequited love. These songs identify the ways that women have devoted their lives to the whims of their fathers, brothers, and husbands. Many women have internalized these messages and the patriarchal norms that they affirm. My analysis shows that if some women refuse to sacrifice their desires and act on the love that the songs evoke, the Zina Ordinance becomes a strategy for their control.

Although the Zina Ordinance was rooted in General Zia's reading of sacred texts, Sara Suleri (1995, 145) suggests that religion was not the only reason that it was implemented in Pakistan. Instead, she points to "the United States government's economic and ideological support of a military regime during that bloody but eminently forgotten decade marked by the 'liberation' of Afghanistan." Indeed, the Pakistani regime under General Zia ranked as one of the top four recipients of American aid (HRW 1992).

General Zia was able to fund his Islamization project with billions of dollars provided by the United States and Saudi Arabia as support for Afghan rebels, many of whom lived and organized in Pakistan (AI 1995; Anwar 1988; Khan 2001a). Pakistan benefited from this military and financial aid in two ways: some of the money was given directly to Pakistan for its help with the Afghan war, and some, marked for Afghan rebels, was siphoned off by Pakistani officials for their personal use. These monies also strengthened religious parties in both Pakistan and Afghanistan. As General Zia was now an ally of the West in its Cold War with the Soviets, few questions were asked about the rise of state-sponsored religious fundamentalism or about the coercive effects of his policies. Indeed, the graduates of *madrassas* (Islamic schools) found employment fighting the Soviets and their client state in Afghanistan, where they became an integral component of a proxy Cold War initiative.

There was no room for a left-inspired politics in the Nizam-e-Mustapha, as Zia accelerated a process, begun by his predecessor, Zulfikar Ali Bhutto, through which the left was largely destroyed. Particularly affected were left-wing student organizations, while those organizations connected to the fundamentalist Jamat-i-Islami were afforded government patronage. Tariq Ali (2002) argues that this process was part of a worldwide effort by the United States to strengthen and use Islamic fundamentalism against left-leaning indigenous movements. Hassan Gardezi (1983) notes that American-sponsored Islamic ideology also provided authoritarian governments with a tool to suppress dissent, and the Zia regime particularly benefited from these policies. Zia promised that "his army will defend both the 'territorial' and 'ideological' boundaries of Pakistan." The latter, Hassan Gardezi (1983, 363) notes, points to the defence of Islam and acts as a euphemism for the repression of political dissenters in Pakistan.

Rouse (1998) points out that Zia gave religious parties a central place in state institutions. At the same time, Islamization effectively increased the state's power over the lives and liberties of its citizens and brought more people, particularly women, into greater contact with what has been described as an abusive and corrupt criminal justice system (HRW 1992). Religiously influenced laws and policies are still in force in Pakistan.[6]

Zia's policies did generate some resistance, particularly from the women's movement.[7] It was not broadly based, however, and Sadia Toor (1997) and Aijaz Ahmed (1983) cite several reasons for this. A series of circumstances benefited the economic and social climate of the period of Zia's regime (1977-88), rendering it a time of relative peace and prosperity. For example, there were several years of good harvests and significant remittances from foreign workers living in the Middle East. Indeed, as Aijaz Ahmed (1983, 136-37) noted at the time, funds flowing from Saudi Arabia (US $2 billion in 1980) "in the form of remittances, [have], until recently, been [a] main element salvaging the foreign exchange situation, even as the domestic structure of the economy has become increasingly hollow and directionless." Zia and his religious supporters attributed the relative affluence of the period to the moral direction provided by Islamization, and few questions were asked about inequalities generated by existing social conditions (Burki 1984). Much of this wealth was not used to build social infrastructure. Instead, it went to purchasing consumer goods, particularly luxury items for the wealthy.

It has been argued that insecurities due to economic and ecological disaster, urbanization, and militarization frequently turn people to politicized religion, which among muslims is often referred to as Islamism (Eickelman 1987; Mernissi 1992). I do not want to conflate Zia's process of Islamization and Islamism; the former was a state policy, while the latter has often been in opposition to the state in Pakistan and elsewhere. Zia's temporary alliances with the fundamentalist Islamist party Jamat-i-Islami helped him politically. Islamization both endorsed and was similar to Islamist programs elsewhere:[8] it focused on a symbolic and moral cleansing, frequently providing simple answers to complex problems.

Notwithstanding his stance on morality and religious piety, General Zia has been criticized as an intolerant and vindictive man who executed the country's elected prime minister (Talbot 1999). Moreover, his Afghan policies resulted in a significant increase in drug trafficking in Pakistan and greater armed sectarian violence due to the large numbers of weapons made available because of the Afghan jihad. Weiss (1986b, 108) notes that Zia's Islamization program did not focus on a "redistribution of wealth, especially of rural land-holdings; establishment of an Islam-based political decision-making process [or] formation of social programs stressing man's obligations to God's creation, *haquq ul-abad.*" Instead, she argues, women were singled out in his reforms, which reinforced the authority of extended families and appeared to favour a more feudal economy. Women were not encouraged to be independent workers. Rather, as the narratives in Chapter 4 of this book suggest, they continue to be socialized as obedient daughters, wives, sisters, and mothers. Nawaz Sharif, Zia's protégé, did little to dismantle Zia's legacy when he came to power. Neither did Benazir Bhutto, who was privately a modernist but publicly emphasized the role of religion and began to dress the part by covering her head.

The connection between religion and nationalism suggests a dimension of the issue particularly relevant to gender struggles. Kumkum Sangari and Sudesh Vaid (1990) note that the politicization of communal and religious identities around ideas of the nation in South Asia has accompanied the impoverishment of women. Such a link, I believe, has significant implications for how the zina laws are enforced in Pakistan. As more and more women suffer the effects of poverty, their bodies, marked through exclusionary practices of class and gender, are rendered the most vulnerable to the zina laws. Indeed, my investigation will show that the Pakistani state appears to lack the means and/or the political will to enforce the laws for any except the most vulnerable citizens: poor women. It is they who largely suffer because of the laws and they who use the contradictory space of their incarceration to pose challenges to the families and the laws that treat them unfairly. Feminists with transnational links can devise and implement interventions that empower these women.

3
Speaking to the Women

Women in Prison

In order to refocus the Orientalist gaze away from viewing non-Western women or Pakistani women as the only ones who are unjustly treated, I draw attention to a global trend. Feminist criminologists (e.g., Comack 2000b; Boyd and Faith 1999; Morris 1987) argue that we should view women's involvement with the criminal justice system as largely a function of their social, political, and economic subordination under patriarchy. Moreover, some point out, women's incarceration is often prefigured by physical and sexual abuse in the home. Studies of Indian prisons, for example, connect sexual abuse to the confinement of many female prisoners. The majority of women in Indian prisons, it is argued (Hazarika 1988), are rape victims who have been placed in "protective custody" in prison to ensure that they will be present at the trial of the accused rapist. The accused rapist, on the other hand, is not apprehended, let alone incarcerated. In her studies of Canadian women's stories of incarceration, Elizabeth Comack (1996, 2000a, 2000b) notes just such a prefiguring and suggests that we view women's encounters with the criminal justice system as an overall policy and practice through which men exercise control over women. There is another aspect to women's imprisonment. Prisons frequently resemble poorhouses. Noted American criminologist Jeffery Reiman (2001) suggests that a person has a greater chance of being arrested and charged if he or she is poor. Money, he argues, provides an enormous advantage to those seeking to manipulate the justice system.

These comments suggest that class and control of women's sexuality appear integrally connected to their incarceration. Field research that I conducted in Pakistan during the period 1998-2002 on the effects of the Zina Ordinance suggests that these views are certainly valid in Pakistan. Here the needs of the state and those of families intersect to create and sustain conditions through which impoverished women spend years in prison for zina.

Accessing the Women

The subjects of my interviews were all incarcerated under the Zina Ordinance when I met with them during my fieldwork in Pakistan. I use the term "met" intentionally because during this period I was not able to speak to the women in private or to conduct an in-depth interview with any of them. I cannot therefore provide a detailed account or present a life story of any of the women whom I met. If such stories had been given central space in this discussion, they would undoubtedly have contributed to a more nuanced analysis. Such a limitation has an unfortunate result: at times during this discussion, I almost end up speaking for them. I want to identify at least two reasons for this significant shortcoming of my study.

First, because of my institutional commitments in Canada, I could not stay in Pakistan for a sustained period, making my research visits there sporadic. During the six-year research span, I visited Pakistan about six times, with each stay being four weeks in length. Perhaps if I had been at my research site for prolonged periods, I could have taken advantage of on-the-spot opportunities to meet with women.

Second, I was unable to locate any woman released from incarceration who could speak to me of her experiences. Indeed, lawyers and other activists who work with women charged under the ordinance could not direct me to former clients who were now out of prison, for they did not know their whereabouts. The process of incarceration, Human Rights lawyer Hina Jilani claims, is extremely destructive for the women. Some of the women go back to their families after they are released from prison. The families protect them from outsiders and at times prevent them from having outside contact.[1] Frequently, their families do not want them back, so the women just disappear and make their lives anew in whatever way they can. Local knowledge suggests that many of these women become prostitutes. However, I have not been able to substantiate this claim.

Although Jilani could not connect me with former prisoners, I was able to find them in the Karachi central jail and in Kot Lakpat prison in Lahore as well as in a state-sponsored women's shelter, or *darul aman* (house of peace). Responding to pressures from nongovernmental organizations (NGOs), the Government of Pakistan has been working to make the prison system more transparent and more accessible since the mid-1990s. Using informal networks, I obtained permission to visit these institutions. On subsequent research trips, the prison authorities became familiar with my project, enabling me to get permission without any help. Perhaps they thought that I posed little threat and could be dismissed if need be as a Westernized academic and therefore irrelevant. In these institutions, I interviewed approximately one hundred and fifty women over the six-year period.

The third reason for my limited access to the women was that I had been warned against private interactions with imprisoned women. The culture of the institutions where I found the women discourages private visits with women. An institutional official is always present. Indeed, Jilani discouraged me from speaking to a woman without an official being present, suggesting that this might have repercussions for the woman after I had left. Even in the presence of the official, Jilani recommended that I not question women openly about their experiences in and out of a prison or a darul aman. Moreover, she recommended that I not ask about experiences of violence that might have been perpetrated in police custody or in the institutions in which they now found themselves. Jilani explained: "Just to ask a[n imprisoned] woman about violence is to expose her to danger. We [the Human Rights Commission of Pakistan] don't know what is happening to her inside. We will leave and she will be left alone. If anyone wants to retaliate, they can do it. This is something we have always discouraged that people should go and ask this question: Has anyone been violent with you?"

This suggestion led me to start the interviews with the question "What events led you to this place?" In this manner, each woman could answer within the confines of what felt safe for her. I interjected only to clarify what she had said. It is very possible that they wanted to say more but did not because they did not feel safe in front of the institutional official or with me, the newcomer. They told their stories without hesitation and doubt as if they had narrated them before.

Not having access to women who were former prisoners and relatively free to speak to the process of incarceration without fear of repercussions left several areas unexplored. What were their experiences in the lockup and in the prison? What kinds of contacts did they have with their families upon release? Were they able to connect with, and regain custody of, their children? What kinds of strategies did they employ to rebuild their lives? These unanswered questions suggest some of the limitations of my investigation while also partly explaining why the victims of zina laws do not offer resistance to the state. They do not, for instance, organize against the law or agitate against the process that treated them so unjustly. Their families silence them, or they purposely vanish. Their disappearance hands the state a clean slate, one on which there are no victims demanding restitution. The few demands for restitution come from legal and editorial challenges by activists and journalists, who are easily dismissed as contaminated by the West.

At Kot Lakpat Prison, Lahore, December 1998

Throughout my visit to Kot Lakpat prison, I was accompanied by Assistant Superintendent Rehana Yasmin. She informed me that 50 percent of the thirty women in the prison are there because of the Zina Ordinance.[2] Women are incarcerated at Kot Lakpat in a separate female compound enclosed by a high wall and are guarded by female guards. This compound, which has a garden and a courtyard, is very clean. There is a play area for children, and Yasmin pointed out that there were about twelve children there at the time. Some of these children accompanied their mothers to jail, as there were no other family members able and willing to look after them. Other children were born to prison inmates. The girls stay with their mothers until the latter are released. The boys, however, are transferred to the juvenile jail on their twelfth birthday.

The women are quartered in large barrack-like rooms and store their belongings, such as pots, pans, and food, under their beds. Although they are provided with food in the prison, they also cook whatever their relatives bring them. Residents who have been there for some time display camaraderie and appear to rely on each other for friendship and support.

The superintendent called in a group of nine women who were in prison for zina-related offences, and the women spoke with me one by one. Although they signed or thumb printed the consent forms, which I had explained to them, I am uncertain whether participation was their choice.[3] I did not question them regarding their participation because I did not want to compromise them. When the superintendent momentarily left the room, several women complained that the female complex had been without water for several days. They asked whether we could use our influence to arrange for them to have water. Their comments reinforced Jilani's view that their remarks were to some extent structured by their inability to speak freely without fear of reprisals.

Of the nine women with whom I spoke at Kot Lakpat, three had been charged as accomplices to runaways, two had been charged as accomplices to abductions, three had been charged with zina, and one had been arrested during a raid at a house of prostitution, where she worked as a maid. One of the women charged with zina stated that she had worked as a prostitute.

At the Darul Aman, Lahore, December 1998

Conditions at the darul aman in Lahore were less transparent than those in the two prisons that I visited. I had less access to the shelter and therefore do not have the same amount of information about conditions there or about the daily routine of the women as I do for the prisons. The darul aman in Lahore is funded by the Anjuman-e-Himayat-e-Islam, a religious organization involved in education and charity work. Women cannot admit themselves to this shelter; they must be referred. While those women who have been charged with zina are sent to jail, in other cases, women who have asked the courts for protection from the violence of their families and current or former husbands have been sent to a darul aman. Zubaida Khatoon, superintendent of the shelter in Lahore claims that she is not allowed to admit women without a reference because the shelter could then be sued or staff harassed by the woman's relatives for taking in "just any woman seeking refuge." These procedures suggest that women at risk need powerful supports in order to be granted refuge in government-sponsored institutions. At the Lahore darul aman, women are charged for food and lodging at the rate of twenty rupees per day, or 8,000 rupees per year. The charges are forgiven, Khatoon claims, if the women cannot pay, and the costs are borne by Anjuman-e-Himayat-e-Islam. However, human rights lawyer Jilani (1998) disputes these claims and argues that it is not easy for women to leave the darul amans. First, they need court orders and, second, the darul amans are quite vociferous in their claims to get money from women who want out of the shelter. Jilani had gone to the darul aman in Lahore with a Supreme Court order to get some women out of the shelter who had indicated to her that they wanted to leave. Khatoon said to her, "We don't accept the Supreme Court Order; just give us the money." Jilani stated, "I did not give them the money; they had asked the wrong person. But I did get the women out." Statements in a Human Rights Watch (HRW 1992) report suggesting that the darul amans function like prisons support Jilani's comments. They are patrolled by armed guards and locked at all times, the report notes. The women are locked in their "cells" at 5:00 p.m. every day and are allowed only one phone call per week. Moreover, some women complained to the HRW of beatings by the institutional staff.

The residents at the darul aman sew and do embroidery, skills that generate some income but likely not enough to provide the economic self-sufficiency required if they are to make substantive changes in their lives. An Amnesty International (2002, 36) report lends weight to this observation, "women sheltering there [in darul amans] are merely shut away and do not acquire, during their period of stay, any proficiencies that would enable them to rebuild their lives outside the shelter."

Some of the women stay at the darul aman a few days, and some stay several years. At the time of my visit, a woman in residence for five years claimed the longest stay. If the women have no place to go, then the Anjuman-e-Himayat-e-Islam will eventually arrange marriages for them. There is no provision in these procedures if attempts at arranged marriages fail. Moreover, Khatoon pointed out that if there is a dispute between a woman and her family, she speaks to both and decides who is telling the truth. If Khatoon believes the woman, she supports her against the wishes of the family. However, if she believes the family, she follows the family's wish, which is usually that the woman be sent home. I asked Khatoon whether being sent home had ever caused problems for women. She responded, "No, because none of them have ever come back to ask for shelter again." Clearly, Khatoon equates women not returning to the shelter with "no problems" at home. The extent to which families abide by decisions made by darul amans or, indeed, by the courts is beyond the scope of this investigation. It is entirely possible that the opinions of shelter officials carry some weight with women's families. However, as an Amnesty International (2002) report indicates there is no evidence of any follow-up by staff at the darul amans to ascertain that a woman has returned to a safe environment. Rather, these adjudications suggest that a woman is without recourse if she loses the option of refuge at a darul aman because its superintendent rules in favour of the family.

There is little regulation of the darul amans by the state. Khatoon's comments support this view and further indicate that the darul amans do not have structured procedures and policies that guarantee women's constitutional rights of freedom and liberty as adults, placing women who have found shelter there at greater risk than those incarcerated in the prison. At the darul aman that I visited, there seems to be no legal or procedural accountability, and Khatoon's discretionary "judging" of the women speaks to this power. Women who are sent home by Khatoon might not always be happily reintegrated into their families. Frequently, families continue to coerce and intimidate them into complying with family wishes. When all else fails, it is commonly believed that disobedient women are killed by their families to reclaim family honour (Bari 2002; CIW 1997).

The darul amans are overcrowded and frequently lack the NGO-run programs in basic literacy and legal awareness that are available in the urban prisons. These conditions led Amnesty International (2002) to suggest that some women prefer to stay in jail. Access to information and to the women was more restricted at the darul aman than at the prison. No one was able or willing to tell me how many women were residing there or how many were there because of the Zina Ordinance. Four women who had been charged under zina laws were brought to speak to me one by one. Jamila Saleem, the assistant superintendent at the darul aman, was present throughout the interviews.

At the Karachi Central Jail, December 1998 to July 2002

The Karachi central jail, like Kot Lakpat prison in Lahore, is primarily a prison for men with a section for juvenile offenders. The women's section is a part of the juvenile jail, reflecting women's status as social minors. Armed guards patrol the entrance. To get inside, you have to knock at the metal gate, at which point a guard opens a square peep hole to see who is there and then decides whether to let you in. Once you step inside, you encounter a man sitting at a table to your right with a register in which visitors sign their names and record the times that they enter and leave the prison. You are then sent to the office of the superintendent, who examines your letter of permission. This is the procedure for the first visit. On subsequent visits, it may be repeated in full or in part or not repeated at all. Once you have gone through this process, you come to the second set of metal doors, where you meet the female warden. She asks whether you have a camera and a mobile phone before conducting a physical search of your body and anything else that you may be carrying. I was searched only a couple of times but was often asked if I had a mobile phone. I had been told by activists that if I entered the premises with a phone and allowed one of the inmates to use it, I would likely be denied entry in the future.

At the Karachi prison, I initially met women in a process similar to the one at Kot Lakpat – a prison official was present at all times. The official informed me that many of the women spent considerable time fighting with each other. She further noted that a lot of them were depressed. There is a health clinic within the women's compound, and numerous women were taking advantage of the antidepressants available for free. This liberal dispensing of antidepressants suggests that the prison authorities are using the drugs as a method of control. The medication seems to have side effects, and a considerable number of the women appeared to have lost interest in prison programs. The inspector general of prisons complained to me that "they are lazy and do nothing all day." Perhaps these factors explain why I was given permission to run a women's group for six months as a means to encourage them to participate in the prison programs. I was also interested in this agenda, as I believed that they would learn skills through these programs that would serve them well in their lives on the outside. But I had other motives as well. I also wanted greater insight into women's lives both in and out of prison, and for this I needed greater access to them. The group met three times a week from July to December 2001. Two research assistants led this group while I was away teaching in Canada. Although the group was to include a prison official, this did not always happen. The prison is short-staffed, so the prison official attended our meetings only sporadically.

When we began the group, I was informed that there were 226 women in the prison, 120 of whom were there on zina-related charges. Prison officials recruited fourteen women to be part of the group, asking them to meet me at 11:00 a.m. one Monday morning. Huma,[4] aged twenty, commented, "We did not know why we had been told to come. We were afraid and we spoke about this to each other. Myself, I could not sleep all night because I was afraid as to what is around the corner for me." Two of the women had been released and another five had joined when we ended the project in December 2001. This group encounter allowed women to work through their depression and to identify opportunities available in the prison that might be of interest to them. Some of the programs available for women in the Karachi jail were similar to those that I had seen in the darul aman at Lahore, sewing and embroidery. However, the prison programs went beyond income-generating skills to include literacy and legal education.

As part of the group process, we stressed respect during the encounter and privacy outside. The atmosphere generated by the group encounter helped women to develop a closer relationship with each other and to find ways to support each other while in prison. Through this group process, I was afforded more extensive insight into the women's lives than would have been possible from a single interview in the presence of officials. But were their stories true accounts of their lives? Not according to Hamida, aged thirty, who had been in prison for fifteen months: "We do not tell our real stories for several reasons. First, no one really wants to hear our full story, as it is a story of pain and being jailed for zina is only part of this story. Even if we tell our true story, no one will believe us. Also our lawyers have told us to tell our stories in a way that it will help us get out of jail. So we change our stories." Hamida's comments suggest that "telling it like it is" is not always helpful. Instead, she identifies a personal narrative that she produced to help her through her legal process and that also gestures to larger survival strategies both in and out of prison.

Some of the women had initially been afraid to join the project. Indeed, sixteen-year-old Saima, with a three-month-old daughter, whom she called *kaki* (little girl), did not want to come to the group meetings. She came, she stated, only because she had been ordered to do so by prison officials:[5]

> I was afraid, I was afraid that the other women would beat me and beat my daughter. At first I sat quietly and did not say anything out of fear. Now I am really glad that I am part of this group. I am really happy that I came here. Being part of the group has given me a place to ask questions. No one has ever asked me what I felt or what I wanted, they just gave orders. Here I can also ask questions and ask the other women how they plan to survive on the outside. I can ask about my lawyer and I can ask about other things such as places to stay at when we leave here. I am really glad that I am in this group. I feel that I have learned a lot ... about how to look after myself and my daughter.

As we wound up the group project, other women echoed Saima's view. They said that it had been a place to which they could come for answers. They wanted it to continue. I suggested that they mention this to the inspector general of prisons, who was the chief guest at a goodbye party organized by the group. The women told the inspector general that they had become stronger because of the group, as the process had allowed them to bond with each other and to take advantage of the programs available to them. Here is what Shano had to say: "We want this group to continue even after we have been released so that other women can also benefit from it." After the inspector general left the party, the women sang songs from Indian and Pakistani films, read poetry that they had composed themselves, and displayed a camaraderie with each other that had allowed them to survive their incarceration. The most popular song at the party was a hindu *bhajan* (devotional song) that promoted the image of woman's beloved as her "prayer and her god." Interestingly, this was sung several times by a woman who had been accused of zina by her former husband. Numerous songs evoked love and romance, "crimes" of which many of these women's families considered them guilty and for which they were paying through loss of their liberty.

Daily Routine of the Women

A day at the Karachi central jail begins at 6:30 a.m. with a roll call, after which the women say their morning prayers. Following prayers, they receive a breakfast of tea and *roti* (bread). The women commented that the tea is weak and cold and the roti cooked unevenly. At 7:30 each morning they are taught the Qur'an by a teacher provided by a religious organization. At 9:30 a second teacher, supplied by an NGO, teaches them basic literacy in Urdu, an optional program run in a one-room classroom. They lunch at 12:30 p.m. and then are given chores that take about an hour and a half to complete. The rotating duties, for which they are not paid, include cleaning the health clinic or other parts of the compound. Later in the afternoon, they have the option to learn tailoring skills and are paid for any piecework stitching that they may do at rates substantially below the standard wage outside the prison.[6] In this case, the woman who teaches tailoring has obtained permission from authorities to give some paid work to the prisoners. These clothes are made on order for local garment producers. I suspect that there is a kick-back involved in this venture as in most ventures dealing with the prison. Because the prison officials are paid extremely low wages, kick-backs and bribes are their only means to put together a living wage. Three times a week, a lawyer employed by a local NGO provides legal education in the afternoon. The women are instructed in their basic legal rights and how to fill out routine legal forms.

The state spends 10.76 rupees (27 cents Canadian) per day on each prisoner's food, which is cooked by the young male inmates of the juvenile jail. The women complained that the juveniles do not know how to cook. The "dal is tasteless and often not cleaned of its pebbles," they complained. Spices that would have added "taste" to the dal are expensive and likely do not fit into the state budget for inmates. The women receive a single large bar of soap per month for bathing, washing clothes (their own as well as their children's), and doing dishes. They also receive a blanket supplied by the state. A few years ago, beds and bedding were donated to the women's prison by an NGO. Since then the prison population has increased, and there are not enough beds to go around, so many woman sleep on the floor, using their blanket as a mattress. It can make for very cold nights in the winter, the women claim. Women with children receive extra rations of powdered milk and cookies. These provisions are supplied by various NGOs. During Ramadan, the muslim holy month of fasting and prayer, the prisoners receive public donations of cooked food, bangles, and henna.

Despite the spartan conditions under which the women live, they noted that, for the first time, they were presented with the choice not to speak to their families. "If a family member comes to see me in prison," Shano claimed, "I can say: 'No I don't want to see him.' This is amazing.

I have never been able to do this before. Also a screen separates us from our visitors. Our family members can no longer beat us if we don't do as they order us to. They just threaten us from the other side of the screen. If we don't want to be yelled at [by them], we just walk away. This is the first time in my life I have had this choice. And I had to come to jail to get this choice."

Frequently, the women are fleeing their families and have no place to go. Pakistan has a weak rehabilitation program, and there is little assistance available to women to facilitate their reentry into society. While they were all praying for an early release, many were terrified that they would have no place to spend the first few nights. Ferozi, aged twenty-five, and her husband were charged by her parents and imprisoned at the same time. She said, "If my husband is released before me, then I am alright. But if God forbid I am released first, I have no place to go. I know that my parents are after me, and this gives me nightmares." Her comments were echoed by several of the women. Many had no place to go and no one on whom to rely outside the prison. Although they had bonded with other women within the prison and more so during meetings of the women's group, they were afraid of helping each other once released. They did not trust the system or the police. They were afraid that somehow they might be implicated in zina or something else and end up in prison again.

The women's compound has barracks within which the women are confined at 4:00 in the afternoon. At this time, all the women are head-counted – "like cattle," one woman noted – and locked up for the night until the morning roll call. There is a lot of noise in the barracks; women fight with each other, and children cry. "It is difficult to sleep at night," Hamida noted. Each barrack has a television, which they use to watch the state-run station, Pakistan Television (PTV). The women commented that they like to watch movies. This entertainment comes with a price: the good woman of Pakistani films frequently shown on television is the obedient daughter and wife. As I will show in the next chapter, the women's narratives suggest that they are struggling with the ideal images of the good woman into which they been socialized. These images also emanate from the movies and television dramas that they watch.

Ferida Sher (1996) argues that patriarchal norms constructed through and reinforced in films instruct women to sacrifice their needs and desires in favour of patriarchy. Only through sacrificing their desires will they find salvation as well as power and influence in society. The self-sacrificing woman, Lala Rukh Khan (1997) notes, is also the good woman of the good-bad binary that dominates Pakistani films. Because of her obedience and her docility, the good woman can at times escape violence from her family and from state institutions.

By contracting marriages of their own choosing or by challenging abusive husbands, many of the women that I spoke to have resisted all that being a good woman implies. In their resistance, they have had minimal, if any, support from sisters, mothers, and others in their families. The women's narratives suggest that although they are not obedient and docile enough to be a good woman, they do not desire to be the bad woman of the films either, the one who has broken the rules or has been made to break the rules through circumstances such as rape. The bad woman of the movies is killed off, commits suicide, or goes insane (Sher 1996). Sentencing bad women to prison on charges of zina is another form of discipline. In all cases, she loses her chance to become a woman of influence within the family, the mother of sons. The women with whom I spoke have been situated as bad women because of their resistance; at the same time, they are still engrossed in filmic scenarios that project these binary messages of good and bad women. Perhaps the women are engrossed in the films without necessarily fully endorsing a conservative reading of the dominant messages emanating from them. This might be similar to their own readings of Islam, which they use to demand their right to choose a life partner. Contrary to those views that promote the Zina Ordinance as just and Islamic, the women said again and again that Islam had given them the right to choose a partner or to walk away from an abusive one.[7] Then again, perhaps they watch movies, their only link to the outside, to help provide them with dreams of different spaces and different relations. And, of course, movies help to alleviate the killing boredom of prison life.

The women with whom I spoke claim that they want to respect their families, but they also want their families to make themselves worthy of this respect. Indeed, the majority of the women claimed that in prison they are not subjected to the hardships and abuse that they faced in their homes. Says Bano, aged eighteen, "We do not have to work as hard here as we do at home. At home there is no rest; we work all the time, and still they beat us and yell at us and abuse us. Here we keep the barracks clean and wash our clothes. When we finish our chores, we have time to do other things and learn to read and write. I am learning tailoring, and I am going to use my skills to support myself and my daughter when I get out [of prison]. At home I had no time to do anything except work for my family; the work was never ending." Bano's comments helped others to talk about a future different from the life that they had left behind, in which they would not be dependent on their families. Like Bano, many Pakistani women are brought up in a state of dependency. These frequently include the elite and educated women who may have careers that enable financial independence. Such women, too, are largely socialized into dependence – so much so that women living alone without the "protection" of family are frequently suspected of illicit behaviour. At the same time, women who step out of line and challenge these dictates can be regulated through charges of zina. These regulations are couched in terms of ensuring the morality of the daughters and wives of the nation. It is to examining these regulations and how women resist them that I now turn.

4
Disobedient Daughters, Errant Wives, and Others

Morally Regulating Women

How can we understand the moral regulation of impoverished Pakistani women through the Zina Ordinance? And how might this regulation serve broader national and political purposes? In order to address these questions, I draw on Phillip Corrigan and Derek Seyer's (1985, 6) argument that the idea of a common collective consciousness of the nation is not a free-floating signifier: it is grounded in relations of domination and subordination. The ways that the state promotes the collectivity reinforces specific notions of what is morally permissible, distinguishing between the licit and illicit. These socially produced notions, Corrigan and Seyer claim, "are simultaneously descriptive and moral." Moreover, they define moral regulation as "a project of normalizing, rendering natural, taken for granted, in a word 'obvious', what are in fact ontological and epistemological premises of a particular and historical form of social order" (4).

Furthermore, Jeffery Weeks (1995, 47) has pointed to the connection between notions of morality and sexual behaviour "to the extent that 'immorality' in the English language almost invariably means sexual misbehaviour." This appears true in Pakistan as well. State prescriptions of morality focus on prescribed sexual conduct, and any deviation (real or imagined) is deemed immoral and criminal. These prescriptions are more stringent and more regulated in the case of women. Drawing upon the work of Michel Foucault, Ann Laura Stoler (1996) has spoken of the ways that bodies are subjugated and identities produced through disciplinary regimes. Narratives of women whom I interviewed for this study suggest that policies and practices connected to the Zina Ordinance serve capitalist and patriarchal interests by regulating gendered and classed bodies in ways that produce docile citizens. Such a process facilitates a transfer of sexuality from the sphere of "family matters" to the public sphere, where it can be shaped to coincide with "national interests." At the same time, the constitution of "the family" appears central to maintaining notions of nation, morality, and social order. In other words, the zina laws allow the state to identify and regulate sexual conduct as a crucial element of creating a just society. Moreover, as Anne McClintock (1995) has noted elsewhere, female respectability appears linked to the middle-class woman. The disease of poverty was especially dangerous in the female body and served to rationalize the policing of boundaries between the ruling class and the immoral poor. These comments are certainly applicable to the women that I interviewed, all of whom were impoverished, suggesting that class is an important aspect of moral regulation.

Although women's kin groups and families are the primary agents of the process of moral regulation, the practices associated with the zina laws confirm state complicity. This complicity, I argue, is not incidental. As individual bodies become the focus of the regulating gaze, discourse promoting morality in Pakistan remains limited to containing illicit sex. At the same time, attention is deflected away from structural issues such as increasing indebtedness and rising militarization, practices that might implicate politicians and state officials. The women charged with zina have resisted these claims on their bodies and have found themselves entangled in a complex web of state incompetence and corruption. I suspect that there are tens of thousands of others who, intimidated by the threat of similar charges, have complied with family wishes. In what ways, then, are bodies of Pakistani women, particularly those who are impoverished, brought into line to serve family needs?

Liberal intellectual traditions, including those of liberal feminism, focus on the abstract universal citizen, rendering the body irrelevant to the social order. Other feminist theorists, however, believe that the body, particularly the female body, is central to building and maintaining a normative society (e.g., Shildrick and Price 1999). For example, radical feminists (e.g., MacKinnon 1989; Rich 1992) have examined how the institutions of heterosexuality regulate and constrain women so that their sexuality services the nation by culturally and biologically reproducing new generations of citizens. Socialist feminists (e.g., Brah 1996; Yuval-Davis 1997) have spoken of how bodies of impoverished classes have been excluded from sites of power through processes that violate their fundamental citizenship rights.

Nira Yuval-Davis (1997) also comments that the state is not the only entity demanding loyalty from and exercising power over women. Kin groups often function in the same way as families in this regard. For example, women are members of national collectivities that grant them constitutional rights of equality and liberty, but, unlike men, they are also subject to special rules as laid out by their community groups. These rules may deny them rights guaranteed by the state. Many scholars have challenged the notion of the abstract individual as Eurocentric and patriarchal, yet Fatna Sabah (1988) has identified a similar trend in muslim societies. According to Sabah, decontextualized Islamic legal discourse defines reality, as it dismisses and devalues all other, including erotic, discourse. Recourse to an embodied normative morality is thus deemed a challenge to the Islamic social order. This is certainly the case with zina victims. They are incarcerated for acting on what they believe are morally acceptable desires, an incarceration which situates them in a legal limbo from which they are ultimately released through the legal system. Although such a process frees them, it still casts a shadow on their morals, as it dismisses their attempts to act on their desires. The women are aware of this, for although they believe that they we will be released, they know that, having been to prison, they are marked women. Their claims to situate themselves as the good woman will forever be mitigated by this fact.

Much of the available literature does not consider these tensions in women's lives. Instead, scholarship on Zina Ordinance largely examines how zina laws blur the line between rape and sex, rendering the victims of rape susceptible to accusations of fornication. Because of the focus on the Zina Ordinance as a law dealing with rape, I expected to hear stories of rape from the women, but I did not. Although rape is a major problem in Pakistan, many rape victims do not press charges because of social and family pressure (HRCP 1997; HRW 1992). Even in cases where they might want to file charges, victims are frequently pressured not to do so because of the fear that zina charges will be brought against them (Mehdi 1997; Jilani 1998). I did not have access to prison records, and I could not verify the women's accounts. But given the level of proof required for successful prosecution of rape (four adult, male, muslim witnesses) and given the consequences for a woman if she is unable to prove rape (admission of illicit sex), I am not surprised that only two of the approximately one hundred and fifty women whom I met/interviewed said that she had been raped.

The zina laws attempt to regulate who can have sex with whom. Yet sex is not the only issue in the women's accounts. They also identify illiteracy and poverty as the reasons for their incarceration. The women whom I interviewed for this project are clear about their desire to control their bodies and opposed to those who lay claim to them. The women as well as their families seek the help of the state. The former want their civic and religious rights, while the latter attempt to use the Zina Ordinance to control the women. Women's accounts suggest that the state has acceded somewhat to both demands. It has helped families to imprison women and has also helped many women to escape their family's clutches.

Although each woman has a unique story of what led to her being charged with zina, certain themes emerge from their accounts. I have identified these women as daughters rebelling against parental authority, wives fleeing current or former husbands, and others who for various reasons have been implicated in zina crimes. Their accounts suggest that many of the young women are deemed immoral by virtue of defying parental wishes. The older women charged with zina offences, on the other hand, are often constructed as errant wives; at the same time, their stories suggest that their current or former husbands are attempting to extort money from them.

Disobedient Daughters

> I married my neighbour. My parents were against the marriage, although my husband had come with a formal proposal and asked for my hand. My parents said they wanted one *lakh* before they gave him permission to marry me.[1] Then my husband sold his land and was willing to give them the one lakh they had asked for. But they still said no. This time they said that he is Punjabi and we are Sindhis,[2] and we are of a different *biradri* [community]. So I ran away with him, and we got married anyway. My parents found us eventually and charged us with zina and both of us are in jail. Now they say "give us the one lakh we asked for, and then we will withdraw the charges." But the money has been spent on hiding from my parents and on lawyers. Now we have no more money. I am afraid that when we [my son, my husband, and I] are released, my parents will find us and kill us.

These comments were made by Naheed, aged twenty-five, who had no formal education. She was charged under the Zina Ordinance and was an inmate of Kot Lakpat prison in Lahore, where I interviewed her in December 1998.

The constitution of Pakistan has a liberal tradition in that it grants rights to all citizens, giving Naheed the liberty to marry whomever she wants. However, the practices associated with the Zina Ordinance override this right and allow her family to intimidate her and have her incarcerated. I do not wish to reinforce a male-female dichotomy by arguing that only women are victimized through the process or that men alone file charges of zina against women. Indeed, in this case, Naheed's husband was also incarcerated for zina. Furthermore, women's narratives identify instances where mothers have initiated zina charges against daughters. Through their connections with their sons and other male family members, older women frequently have significant status in their families and communities. These arrangements help to identify the ways that women and men strategize within a set of concrete constraints that reveal and define the blueprint of what Deniz Kandiyoti (1988) has termed "a patriarchal bargain" within society. Nevertheless, I do want to identify Naheed as more vulnerable than her husband in this process because of the gender bias in Pakistani law (Jahangir and Jilani 1988; Mehdi 1997; Shaheed 1997b), a bias also present in other countries (Hazarika 1988; Comack 2000a).

My research suggests that about half of the zina-related charges are laid by families against daughters who have married of their own free will. Fathers, brothers, grandparents, and at times mothers have gone to the police and complained that their daughter has been abducted. The husband of the young woman is named as abductor. This occurs even though many of these couples have a *nikhanama* (marriage certificate) proving that they are indeed married. Nevertheless, they are formally charged, and a first investigation report is drawn up, after which they are incarcerated pending trial.

Drawing on the work of Claude Levi-Straus, Gayle Rubin (1975) has pointed out in another context that marriages are a form of exchange between kin groups and that women are seen as a precious gift. This gift allows kin groups to build alliances and to become related to each other by blood. Women are not partners in these exchanges and cannot benefit from their circulation. Rather, as Rubin points out, the benefits are enjoyed by the families. Comments from women whom I interviewed suggest that similar transactions have taken place in Pakistan. Families with little means to cope with increasing inflation and chronic unemployment often find that their daughters' sexuality is a valuable asset, a commodity commanding a high price. Marrying her to the highest bidder in exchange for a "gift" frequently becomes one method of paying off debts. Furthermore, many women are sold into marriage to sustain alcohol and drug habits of their male relatives. Indeed, the women with whom I spoke cited increasing poverty and family violence as the reasons for their plight.

Gulbano, aged fifteen, had completed tenth class and had been in the darul aman at Lahore for six months. Her comments suggest that she is unwilling to allow further commodification of her body:

> Father married me to a man who[m] I like and am happy with and he is close in age to me. He is twenty-two years old. Father and mother used to fight. He left the family and the country. I don't know where he is. No one knows where he is. Now mother wants me to divorce my husband. She says that I am only fifteen and a minor and that she has authority over me. She wants me to marry someone who has promised her money. So my mother has charged us with zina and my husband with abduction. My marriage has been registered, and my husband has the nikhanama. I am happy with my husband, and I do not want to leave him. Twice I have been to court. In the court I was told that I am a minor and should go and live with my mother and do as she says. But I refused. Finally, I came to [the] darul aman. I am afraid of my mother; she has threatened me.

Gulbano's account challenges the notion put forward by some feminist theorists that it is only men who control women and deny them their rights. Instead, her narrative makes a case for an analysis identifying the complexities of the patriarchal bargain. In this instance, Gulbano's mother does not have a nurturing relationship with her; instead, she attempts to commodify her daughter's body. Several of the women commented that their mothers had sided with their fathers in oppressing them, although a few pointed out that their mothers did so out of fear.

Gulbano is a Pathan, and the money promised her family in exchange for her in marriage is known as the "bride-price." Its payment is common practice among Pathans, particularly those living in rural areas. In such cases, Shaheen Sardar Ali (2000, 176) points out, "a woman's consent and/or participation in drawing up of her marriage contract is considered of no consequence. She is bartered away at a suitable bride-price." However, both Sardar Ali and Esposito (1982) argue that this practice manipulates the Islamic requirement of dower.[3] The monies that are agreed upon as dower are to be paid to the woman and are supposed to provide a safety net for her in time of need. Parents accept this money from the husband, a practice facilitated by the fact that the often very young girls who are about to be married are in no position to make claims on it. Dower then becomes a form of payment for the bride, which is given to the parents. Through the payment of this bride-price, women become property to be bought and sold. Young girls are socialized into this practice. Many do not resist, and those who do frequently face accusations of violating the zina laws.

If a woman marries, it must be with parental consent, and the zina laws are a powerful means to secure this consent. If a woman does not have her parents' blessings when she marries, she can be intimidated with the threat of being accused of zina violations. And if this doesn't bring her in line with her parents' wishes, she can be charged and incarcerated under the laws.

Anita Weiss (1986a) comments that the Zina Ordinance reinforces the notion of woman as familial property. Through the process of incarceration, the state colludes in a process that helps families to lay claim to the bodies of their women. Yet, paradoxically, prison and shelters become contradictory places of empowerment where women reject the claims of their families. Salima, aged twenty, who has no formal schooling, had been in the darul aman at Lahore for six months. She, too, wants to use the contradictory space of the darul aman as a space of possibility.

> My mother and brothers threw my stepfather out of the house. They also used to beat me and emotionally and verbally abuse me. They wanted to marry me to a man who already had two children. They owed money to him, and they wanted me to marry him so he would forgive their debt. But I refused. And they beat me more. So I ran away and stayed with a friend for four days. I hid in her balcony, and her parents did not know I was in the house. In those days, I had no food, only what my friend was able to sneak in, mostly tea and some bread. My friend was afraid of her family finding out.
>
> Then I went and stayed with some cousins. They did not keep me either. They are afraid of my mother and brothers and did not want to get involved. But they did give me five hundred rupees and sent me here to [the] darul aman. I don't want to go home. I want to live with my aunt [father's sister], and she says that she will take me. My mother and brothers have told me that if I don't come home, they will charge me with theft and zina. Mother has already made comments about the brother of my friend who sheltered me. She says that maybe I did zina with him. As yet, they have not formally charged him, but I won't be surprised if they do that. My mother says that maybe I also did zina with my stepfather and zina with my cousin. I have no lawyer, and I have no money. If I go home, they will kill me. I am happy here, and I will live out my life in [the] darul aman if I have to. I will show my family that I can survive.

Salima's mother came to visit her during my visit to the darul aman at Lahore. "With a mother like you, who needs an enemy," Salima yelled at her. "You have come here so you can take me home and beat me into submission. I will never go with you, never, you are a liar and a fraud." Salima's comments indicate that she feels safe enough in the shelter to confront her mother and express her rage about her mistreatment at home.

There are verses in the Qur'an that grant equal status to men and women; there are also those that impart to women the status of minors under the control of their families and guardians. Many of these later verses have influenced *sharia* (Islamic religious law). For example, under the Hanafi version of sharia commonly used in Pakistan,[4] fathers and grandfathers contract marriages for minors that cannot be annulled at puberty. John Esposito (1982) argues that this power is not supported by any verse in the Qur'an or by the Sunna. Furthermore, if the minor's marriage has been contracted through fraud or by someone other than the father or grandfather (including the minor's mother), Esposito points out, the minor can repudiate the marriage upon attaining puberty.

The religious sanctions notwithstanding, the Hanafi reading of the sacred texts used in Pakistan allows parents to contract a marriage for a minor daughter, whose sexuality thereby becomes a commodity that can be sold. Often parents contract such marriages for adult children as well, marriages that Pakistani courts have upheld as legal. Hina Jilani (1998) argues that the courts have given contradictory rulings on this matter, at times siding with the parents against their children who have reached the age of majority and at other times validating the decision made by adult children to contract their own marriages. A recent court ruling, however, rendered valid a marriage contracted against the wishes of the parents by a woman who had reached the age of majority.[5] Under such conditions, women who are illiterate or who have little knowledge about the law or what is allowed in Islam are unlikely to appeal legal decisions, particularly since their poverty makes access to the law difficult. If they decide to resist anyway, charges under the zina laws bring them into greater contact with the police force and a legal system known for their corruption. Indeed, a recent survey found that out of twelve selected government agencies, the police were deemed the most corrupt, followed by the lower courts, the two agencies that women will likely come into contact with in the process of incarceration (Ghausi 2001).

The use of zina laws to prosecute and intimidate daughters who have married without parental permission suggests that parental rights override men's rights or claims to their wives. Often young men are as powerless as young women to decide their destiny. These laws particularly control men of underprivileged classes, as they have little access to legal protection. Victims of the Zina Ordinance are not limited to muslims. The narrative of Nausheen, aged twenty, suggests that christians are not exempt from the excesses of these practices. Both she and her husband are christians and have suffered under the law. Nausheen, who had completed ninth class had been at Kot Lakpat prison for three months and was expecting her first child at the time of the interview. She recounted, "I married against my parents' will and they accused my husband of abducting me. And both of us are in jail. My husband is my cousin [son of mother's brother]. I had asked my parents for permission to marry him, but they said no. I got married anyway. And my parents registered a case of zina against us."

Nausheen has a nikhanama to prove that she is indeed married. Her situation, however, suggests that having this official document is insufficient. She claimed that her father, as *wali* (guardian), refused to sanction the marriage. Moreover, her parents have bribed the officials who performed and registered the marriage to say that no marriage exists. They insist that her marriage certificate as well as her marriage is a fraud. Now Nausheen and her husband have to appear in court to argue their case before the judge. This is hampered by the fact that they have little money with which to pay for a lawyer. Court dates are notoriously difficult to get in the overburdened system. The couple may have to wait in jail for months before they appear before a magistrate. If they had been charged in a rural court, their situation might have been worse – as was the case with Rubina.

Although she is fortunate to have a legal-aid lawyer, Rubina's case has been registered in Thatta, where there are no jail facilities for female prisoners. I met her in the Karachi jail, to which she had been transferred and where she was awaiting a court date. Rubina has a certificate to prove that she is indeed divorced from her first husband, who charged her with committing zina with her current one. In order to present this evidence in court before a judge, she has to deal with several factors. She has to wait for a female guard to come and escort her to Thatta. Often these guards do not appear at the appointed time; Rubina has missed two courts dates, six months apart. When the guard finally arrived to escort Rubina to the court in Thatta, the judge did not show up due to illness. Gurmat, aged sixteen, faced with similar circumstances, commented, "What a nonsense system this is; first we wait for the female guard, then we wait for the judge, all to show them our papers. Who designed this system?"

The trip to the courts is also quite stressful for the women. They commented that the guards who came to fetch them try to extort money at every turn. If they bought food to eat during the trip to the court, they also had to buy food for the guards. The guards also wanted bribes before they would allow them to speak to friends and relatives who had come to the court to support the women. Shano, aged twenty-two, and her husband are both in jail and had their court dates on the same day. As there are no daycare facilities in the prison, Shano brought her child along: "My husband wanted to hold our son, but the guard wanted money. Imagine, the guard said, 'I want two hundred rupees before I allow him to hold the child.'"

In addition to the corruption of the guards, the space of the court itself is not woman-friendly. The women complained that the courtroom – indeed, the whole compound where the court is located – was a male space. The only women present there were a few of the lawyers and, of course, the prisoners and their supporters. Sajida, aged thirty-two, commented, "I am not used to being in a place with so many men. I have had very little contact with men that I do not know or am not related to. The men at the courts undress us mentally. I do not feel comfortable there at all." These views were shared by many of the women. To prepare for the courts, many of the women dressed down for the event. However, the women commented that some women dressed up in their best clothes and makeup when they went to court. These comments reveal a desire to perform a middle-class feminine respectability as well as the belief of some women that their sexuality might help them through this difficult process.

I could certainly relate to women's discomfort in the courts. I, too, felt extremely uncomfortable during my visit to the courts. The women there appeared divided into two categories: the lawyers, who wore a white *shalwar-kamez* (loose pants and top), and the prisoners and their relatives, many of whom were veiled or had covered their head with a chador. I did not fit into any of these categories and was therefore stared at more than the other women, to the extent that the judge asked my research assistant (a lawyer who represented one of the women that I was interviewing) who I was and what my business was in the courts. She replied that I was there to assist her. I vowed that, if I had to go to the courts again, I would certainly find a *burkha* (veil) to wear.

The women whom I interviewed are well aware of the challenges they face. They are conscious of being painted as immoral, loose, and promiscuous. Salima, aged sixteen, pointed out that the only immorality of which she is guilty is going against her family's wishes. At the same time, she commented, "My religion allows me to marry who[m] I want." Salima and many of the other women disobey familial demands and desire relationships of love and romance. They believe that they are being punished for their disobedience. Many turn to the law for protection; however, their lack of resources limits their access.

All the women whom I interviewed have been without financial and other resources, suggesting that women with such resources are able to post bail and are now free. Moreover, several well-publicized cases suggest that things happen differently in more influential families. For example, Saima Waheed's court challenge helped to construct the legal definition of a sui juris, or independent, adult female capable of entering into a marriage contract.

The Saima case, as it was popularly known, illustrates the extent to which a woman with material resources can pose legal challenges when faced with ambiguity about her status in the law (Sardar Ali 2000). The common understanding of the Hanafi school of Islamic law, to which the majority of Pakistanis adhere is that a muslim woman has the right to enter a marriage of her own accord. It is not lawful for a guardian to force into marriage an adult woman against her consent. However, this view does not always translate into legal practice, for Pakistani courts have given contradictory rulings on this manner. At times, they have sided with the woman by upholding her right to make her own marriage choices; at other times, they have sided with the parents and stated that her wali's right supersedes her own. There appears to be no pattern to the varying readings of the law.

It was against this backdrop that the Saima case unfolded. Saima came from an upper-middle-class family. She married against their wishes, while her father stated that, as wali, he had the right to forbid the match. When she took up residence in a women's shelter managed by a nongovernmental organization (NGO), her father filed criminal charges against the refuge and accused the administrators of abducting his daughter. Saima petitioned the court, stating that she, as an adult woman, could enter into a marriage contract on her own without the approval of her wali and requested a declaration upholding her marriage. Her case raised several important issues: Is marriage, indeed, a civil contract in Islam? If yes, then in order to enter into this contract, does she have to be sui juris? Moreover, how does the will of her wali enter into this contract? Although Saima was finally deemed an adult capable of entering into a marriage contract, Justice Ihsan-ul-Haq Chaudhary, in a dissenting opinion, argued that "although the free consent of a woman forms an essential element of a valid marriage, this consent is qualified by the overriding right of the *wali* or marriage guardian to withhold or accord assent" (Sardar Ali 2000, 161).[6]

Saima Sarwar and Uzma Talpur's stories also provide examples of how class enters into this process. These women, like Saima Waheed, also came from wealthy families whose influence with authorities denied their daughters the relative safety of institutions (AI 2002). Saima was murdered in her lawyer's chambers in front of witnesses for the "crime" of seeking a divorce from a brutalizing husband against the wishes of her family. Her murderers have as yet not been charged. Instead, her father, a member of the Peshawar Chamber of Commerce, has used his influence to have a *fatwa* (religious decree) issued against her lawyer, Hina Jilani. The second woman, Uzma Talpur, married against her family's wishes and has since disappeared, a disappearance popularly believed to have been orchestrated by her family. Both cases illustrate how wealthy families are able to keep their daughters out of prison and thus within the reach of their vengeance.[7]

The process of being charged and incarcerated appears to politicize some of the women, who begin to question one of the basic tenets of their socialization: obedience to parents. Some women, however, accept the validity of family demands and challenge them at the same time. One woman's predicament provides an example of this contradiction. Aged eighteen, Amina, who had been in prison for eight months, expressed some paradoxical views. She deserved to be in prison, she claimed, for "I married against my parents' wishes, and I hurt them." But at the same time, she rebelled against parental authority by refusing to acquiesce to familial demands that she make a statement claiming that her husband abducted her and forced her into marriage. As she claims her right to choose her marriage partner, Amina also claims her agency. But she pays a price: incarceration in jail.

Although Amina's family is responsible for the charges that resulted in her being incarcerated, they have also been sending provisions and clothing to her in the prison. "My family will support me. I do not need to learn any skills, as my father used to buy me everything I needed when I lived at home. Now that I am in jail, members of my family purchase for me what I need." At the same time, she noted that her father had come after her with a gun when she married a man of her own choosing. Her comments elicited laughter from the older women, Hamida and Rubina, who pointed out that her family is providing for her because they want to be able to control her again. They noted that it was Amina's father who had put her in jail. When she gets out and still refuses to obey her father, maybe he will no longer purchase her clothes, and maybe she should learn to be self-sufficient by taking training in sewing so that she can sew her own clothes or sell them for money. "You might need to support yourself later on in life," Rubina noted. She herself has worked as a seamstress and done embroidery to support herself all her life. Even in prison she draws on these skills to support herself. She is paid fifty rupees for sewing a shalwar-kamez. Some days she sews two suits.

Amina, on the other hand, does not know how to sew or embroider, nor does she know how to read. She knows only how to do housework. Amina did not feel the need to acquire skills and become self-supporting. She claimed that she was not angry with her family and not even angry when her father started shooting at her. Amina disobeyed familial authority and married a man of her own choosing, yet she still desires familial love and support.

Errant Wives

While parents attempt to reign in disobedient daughters through the Zina Ordinance, husbands also find that these laws work in their favour. Husbands chastising or exploiting their former or current wives appear to instigate the second most common (mis)use of the ordinance. Moreover, religion, custom, and illiteracy interconnect to further exacerbate the situation. In Islam, marriage is a civil contract, for the Qur'an (Ali 1968, ll: 282) recommends that the contract be put in writing: "Disdain not to reduce the writing of [your contract] for a future period ... It is more just in the sight of God, more suitable as evidence, and more convenient to prevent doubts among yourselves." This does not often happen in Pakistan (Jilani 1998). Frequently, the husband repudiates his wife, as allowed by sharia. That is, he verbally divorces her in front of three male witnesses. This is a widespread practice in Pakistan, particularly in the rural areas. The divorce, however, may not have been registered with the district council as required by civil law. Since the divorce is not registered, it is invalid. Nevertheless, on hearing her husband repudiate her, a woman commonly believes that she is indeed divorced. She returns home, and her family often pressures her to remarry. If she does so, she can be – and often is – threatened with zina charges by her former husband, who appears asking for money. If the attempt at extortion fails, he frequently files a first investigation report (FIR) with the police claiming that she is his legal wife and has remarried without obtaining a valid divorce. In such a case, the police arrest the woman and her current husband and put them in jail, where they remain until their case comes to trial. This may happen within six months or take as long as five years. It depends on how literate the couple are and how much money they have.

Nusrat, aged twenty-six, had been in the Karachi central jail for one year when I met her in December 2001. Her comments reveal that even compliant women are not safe from the exploitation that frequently accompanies the application of this law:

> My husband, Ahmad, used to come [home] late at night, and sometimes he never came home at all. When I asked him about it, he beat me. He told me that he did not like me and beat me. One day, he beat me so badly that I had to have stitches on my forehead and my nose. Then he pronounced *talaq* [divorce] three times and said: "You are no longer my wife. I have divorced you. If I see you in my house again, I will kill you." So I took my three children and went home to my parents.
>
> My parents are old, and they do not have much money. In the house, only my brother was working, and he has four children. So they all began to pressure [me] to marry again. And eventually I married again to a man they found for me. Amin, my new husband, he was good to me and my children. For a while I was happy. Then my first husband, Ahmad, came back and said that we are not divorced, [that] he has not registered our divorce with the local council, and [that] I am committing zina with Amin. He went to the jail and launched an FIR against us, and now we are all in jail, Amin, the children, and I, too. He [Ahmad] is greedy; they are his children ... for the sake of money, his actions sent his own children to jail. Now Ahmad wants money before he withdraws his case. He wants one lakh. We are poor people, where will we get that kind of money? I do not understand why we are in jail. I did everything Ahmad wanted. I even left the house when he told me to go. I did everything my parents wanted. I married the man they found for me when Ahmad divorced me. I do not understand why we are in jail.

Hamida, aged thirty-three, also suffers because her divorce was not registered. She has been in prison for fourteen months and does not know where her children are. Here is her story:

> I came to Pakistan from Bangladesh when I was nine years old. I came with my sister, who was eleven at the time. Our parents had sent us here with a man who told them that he had work for us. He also gave my parents six months' income in advance. My parents believed him. They are poor with eight other children. They needed the money, and

> they believed him. When we reached Pakistan, he married me off to a man who gave him money, and I had three children. My husband was much older than me, and he died when I was eighteen. Soon afterwards my sister also died. She had been married off as soon as we arrived and had four children by the time she died. These children were left in my care, and now I had seven children to look after. Her husband began to pressure me to marry him, and so finally I did. I thought that, as a single woman, how would I support these seven children? I would need the help of a man. But the bastard gave me little support. He barely kept a steady job. I worked as a cook during the day and came home and looked after the house and the children. He also abused me and tried to molest my daughter. I married her off, after which he began to abuse me even more. One day, he divorced me in front of the neighbours. Now I have been told that it was not a legal divorce because it was not registered, but at the time I thought that I was truly divorced.
>
> So after three years, I married for the third time. Now my second husband, Moen, has charged me with zina. He says that I am legally still married to him, as he never registered the verbal talaq. I married for the third time, as I wanted the support of a man, and look what I got, jail. What is worse is that Moen has run off with the children. I don't even know where they are or what condition they must now be living in. If I find him, I will skin him alive.

Hamida's story is complex and hints at the ways that globalization has impoverished families so that they barter away daughters for wages or "sell" them into marriage. The young women, some of them children find themselves without the support of kin networks in a new environment where they are at the mercy of men whom they do not know. Their fate is largely dependent on the character and goodwill of husbands, to whom the Zina Ordinance gives extraordinary power. As the stories of both Hamida and Nusrat suggest, in a woman's life, a husband can come and go at will. He can control her, but she has no claims on him. His actions suggest a form of patriarchal ownership made more concrete by zina charges.

Paradoxically, husbands use the threat of zina to intimidate their wives as well as to compel them to commit zina as a source of income. Like Naheed, Rashida Bibi, aged eighteen, is also from Sindh, where they demand a bride-price. She had no formal education and had been at the darul aman in Lahore for four months. Here is what Rashida Bibi had to say: "Father owed money to an old man. And he married me again to the old man. My new 'husband' not only slept with me, but also made me commit zina with six other men in exchange for money, which he kept. And he also beat me and broke my arm. He had a first wife, who was also involved in prostituting me, and she also beat me. I registered [a] case of rape against the old man and his wife with the police. I am in [the] darul aman because the old man's son-in-law has threatened me. My father also used to beat me."

Many of the women were quite clear about demanding their rights. Rubina, aged thirty-six, pointed out, "Allah gave us the right to marry whom we want and [our] parents try to take this right away from us ... Our parents are sinners, not us." While the majority of the women were clear that they were in the right in making their life choices, to some extent they were still drawn to the idea that their families, particularly their husbands, would support them in their daily struggle to survive. When asked "How many of you have had the support of a man?" almost all of the women in my discussion group at the Karachi central jail responded with laughter. Most commented that they had never had support from the men that they married. On the contrary, it was they who had supported their husbands. Indeed, several women had been told by their husbands to bring in income to support them and their families by begging. Their husbands meanwhile did nothing. Some used their wives' income to gamble and take opium, leaving hardly enough funds to feed the children. Mansoora, aged forty, had lost an arm in a factory accident ten years ago. Her husband said she should capitalize on her disability and forced her to beg. When she did not bring in enough to support his drug habit, he beat her and said, "I don't care what you do just bring in money." She exclaimed "He even wanted me to commit zina for money. When I refused, he charged me with zina, and here I am."

Conventional views of family suggest that these women's families, husbands, and children will give them *sahara* (material and emotional support). Thus the good woman is the one who, having sacrificed all for the family, receives sahara. The process of incarceration complicates these views. Comments from some of the women suggest that, although their families and husbands want them to obey the rules and labour for them, there is no payoff. That is, they are not willing to provide support for the women in return. Indeed, comments made by ten of the fourteen women in the group, who were older than the others, reveal that they do not believe that anyone will support them and that they must learn to support themselves. At the same time, the four younger women indicated that, despite their experiences, they still desire this support. Shano, aged twenty-two, who has an eight-month-old son, pointed out that her husband never had an opportunity to demonstrate that he would give her sahara. They were together only one month before they were both charged and jailed. The charges were on the basis of an FIR launched by her parents for marrying against their will. Huma, aged 20, who has a five-month-old child, had been with her husband only ten days, and Gurmet, aged 16, had been with her husband only two weeks. All three women still held out hope that their husbands would support them, although they were quite clear that their families would not do so.

Others Implicated in Zina Cases

The moral regulation of women through the Zina Ordinance reveals the extent to which docile middle-class women are considered moral, while agentive, impoverished women are deemed immoral. These constructions are also influenced by everyday verbal and textual conversations of middle-class women regarding the loose, sexual, promiscuous lower-class woman, whose sexuality is running wild and needs to be controlled. Poor people who have large families are blamed for the population explosion and are routinely targeted by population-control schemes. Issues left unexplored in such analyses include the ways in which the poor rely on children to provide social security in old age and the extent to which parents' insufficient wages force them to depend on the income of their children.

Women's narratives suggest that applying zina charges helps to provide families with docile daughters, mothers, and wives. A threat of zina charges might also be utilized to provide docile workers, although I found little evidence of this in the women's narratives. There is tremendous potential for abuse of women. Outspoken women, those who challenge authority or who organize other women into unions, might also be brought into line, and intimidated into accepting difficult and poorly paid work because they fear zina charges. These are exactly the kind of workers that multinational corporations are looking for when they invest in a country.

Feroza Bibi's story provides an example. She is fifty years old, has no formal education, and had been in prison for a year. Feroza did not work for a multinational corporation; her account, however, reveals the extent to which employers can use charges of zina for their own advantage. The woman for whom she worked appeared to draw on conventional occupational stereotypes of the domestic servant as immoral and unreliable to sanction and persecute Feroza as an undesirable. Her crime was not that of committing zina but of helping to facilitate the immorality of a younger woman. While promoters of the zina laws use Islam to justify them, Feroza Bibi's narrative suggests that she uses the same religion to comfort herself in prison:

> I used to work as a sweeper [a day worker] at a house. I worked there for eight months, one hour every day, and [I] received three hundred rupees [Cdn $6.00]. One day my mistress complained that "your work is not good." I said, "But the work that I do for you is good work." Then she beat me, and I ran away to my village. I was afraid that she would accuse me of theft. I was too afraid to ask for wages that were owed me. Another girl also worked for the mistress, and she ran away. The mistress told the police that I had helped her run away. And they registered a case of zina against my husband and I. The police came to our village and brought us to jail. Now my husband and I are both in jail. No one comes to visit us. My older children have also been implicated by Mistress and Master, and they are afraid to come and see their parents. Who will be my *vakil* [lawyer]. Allah is my vakil. Maybe Allah will have pity on me since it is Ramazan [or Ramadan, the muslim holy month of fasting and prayer].

Hina Jilani (1998) argues that once a case has been initiated and a first investigative report launched, police are "under pressure to tie up the investigation and send the case for prosecution." Police performance is evaluated annually. Unresolved cases, Jilani points out, reflect poor police performance. Thus police are often looking for a victim. Poor women with few resources are also ideal victims for the police who want a tidy conclusion to cases. Naseem Jehan, aged forty-nine, had been in Kot Lakpat prison for seven months. Her story provides an example:

> My neighbour, who is also my relative, well, her daughter-in-law ran away. And I was accused of helping her run away. The mother-in-law of the girl accused me of being an accomplice. She wanted money from me. I have been accused of a crime that I have not committed. They [the courts] are asking three lakhs for bail. I have sold everything, even my jewelry, to support my case. My eldest daughter is sixteen, and she is alone at home with my husband. My husband has a bad temper, and I am afraid for her. My bail has been raised three times and is now three lakhs. Because the judge also wants money. I am against judges. Please write "against judges."

Jehan's comments are supported by Zakia's remarks. Zakia, aged twenty-eight, is from Okara District. She had no formal education and had also been in prison for seven months.

> I had a fruit shop in Lahore. I had employed a boy to work for me. He abducted his cousin, and I got charged with helping in the abduction. There is no one to bail me out as my husband has also been charged and is also in jail. The police said that he gave the couple a ride in his vehicle. I have been told that the abducted girl testified against my husband and me. I do not know what was said in the police station. I do not understand. I have no lawyer. I have four children; their ages are four years, six years, nine years, and ten years. They are with my uncle right now. Sometimes I write letters to them. And sometimes I get letters from them.

Zakia's narrative identifies dispersal of a family because of zina charges. Even when she is released through the court system, her family will likely be traumatized by the process.

Parveen's family has also faced considerable trauma. Her comments indicate that women escaping violence in the home are made vulnerable to violence of the police through the Zina Ordinance. Parveen, aged twenty, had never been to school but knew how to read and write Urdu. She was married with a seven-year-old son and had been at Kot Lakpat for nineteen days.

> My brother Mustafa is married to Razia, and Razia has a sister, Rukaya. Now Rukaya and her husband fought a lot. He used to bring home other women, and when Rukaya complained, he beat her. At one time, Rukaya jumped into the river with her daughter and attempted suicide. A man who was passing by saw them and pulled them out. When her husband beat her, Rukaya went home to her parents, and sometimes she went to her sister Razia's house. When Rukaya finally ran away, she came to Razia's house. And Razia told her that "although others close their doors against you, I will always keep my door open for you."
>
> We were afraid, my parents were afraid, and I was afraid. And [we] suggested to Mustafa that he leave Rukaya with her parents. We were afraid that there would be trouble. But he refused and allowed Rukaya to stay in their home. Rukaya was also afraid that her husband would come looking for her [at] Razia's house, so she ran away from there [as well]. And her husband did come looking for her. He said that Razia, her husband, and his family had abducted his wife. So now the whole family is charged with abduction and helping Rukaya run away. They are all in jail, my father, and my three brothers. I am in jail. Razia is also in jail. Rukaya has disappeared, and Razia fears that her in-laws have abducted her; otherwise, she would be in touch with Razia. Rukaya's brother and husband say that they will kill her if she turns up. We are

> poor, and they are rich. Razia's husband does not want to blame his wife. But the rest of the family blames her. I blame her for bringing so much misfortune to our family.
>
> This case was registered two months ago. The police took my brothers into the lockup and beat them up. They beat them a lot, and they have a lot of bruises. They took money from us. I have no one to bail me out; all my three brothers are in jail, and my father is jail. I don't know where my husband is. My son is with my mother, and I have left everything to Allah.

Like Parveen, forty-year-old Sajida has had no formal education. Her narrative indicates that poverty and illiteracy contributed to her imprisonment. She has four children, whose ages range from sixteen to twenty-one. She had been in prison for eight and a half months. "A lady doctor lived near us who did abortions. She said to me, 'if you bring me clients, I will do free treatment for you and give free medicine [to you].' I have kidney and asthma problems and do not have the money for medical treatment. So I brought her clients. I brought her an unmarried girl who was pregnant and who wanted an abortion. She ran away after the abortion, and her family registered an FIR and blamed me as an accomplice. Now the police have accused me of abducting the girl."

Farida's story also identifies cruel and corrupt police practices. She is from Kasur District, has had no formal education, and has been at Kot Lakpat for twenty-two days:

> My husband's younger brother was getting married. I had come to Lahore on my way to Islamabad for the wedding. I was at the Lahore station waiting to take the coach to Islamabad. I sat down at a table to have tea, and a man sat down at the same table to have tea. The police came and accused us of zina. They said that you have booked a room at the hotel for zina. And I said that I have never even thought of this. They arrested me and also arrested the man. We are both in jail. I have five children; their ages are one, two, four, six, and eight years. The youngest one is with my mother, and the rest are with my husband.[8] My husband believes me and thinks of me as a "*gharaloo*" [domesticated] woman. But we have no money and no property to register. And we can't pay bail.

Firdaus, also aged thirty-five, has no formal education. She is married but did not know where her husband was. Firdaus lived with her parents and her two sons, who are nine and thirteen years old. Here is what she had to say:

> I worked as a cleaner at the home of a former madam. There was a raid at the house, and the police caught me. I am not sure why. I have no lawyer. My parents, they know I worked but don't know I am in jail. My parents think I am away on work. Now it is two months since I saw my parents, and they and my children must be worried. I have no lawyer. I can't tell my parents I am in jail. They are too old and will die of shock and shame. I hope that someone will come forward and pay my bail. I have asked other women if they know someone who will help. I will pay them back. If you know someone, please help me. I have no one. I am *sharif* [honest]. I will pay them back. That is all I can do. How much will it cost about two or three thousand. It can't be more. I am strong and healthy. I will work and pay it back.

Farida's and Firdaus' narratives identify poverty as the overriding factor in their disempowerment. Their accounts also speak to a lack of access to basic citizenship rights by poor and agentive women, who are largely seen as immoral.

Women's stories speak of physical and emotional abuse; they do not speak of sexual abuse. This is because, should they accuse someone of rape and if they lack the sufficient evidence to prove it, they will likely face zina charges. Sixteen-year-old Salima faced such charges. She was abducted from her parents' home and kept confined in an isolated location by a local landlord. He raped her, and she got pregnant. When Salima attempted to file rape charges against him, the local police station refused to file an FIR; instead, they accused Salima of lying. Through the intervention of a military officer, Salima was fortunate enough to get an FIR launched against her abductor. He proposed marriage, a proposal that she refused. "I fear for my life if I am married to him," she explained. Salima's allegations of rape were taken as testimony that sexual intercourse had occurred, and she was charged with zina. She is now in prison, and he is on the outside. Salima's parents have tried to have her released on bail, but she refuses to go home. She claims that her father used to beat her, and she likes the safety of prison, commenting "No one beats me here." Her account reveals the contradictory nature of the space of imprisonment; while it confines women, it also protects them from some forms of male violence.

A formal reading of the law makes prostitutes, who have sex outside of marriage, the most likely victims of these laws. My research reveals that this is not always the case. Comments made by Najma Parveen (1999) support my findings. Parveen notes that many prostitutes have powerful connections who not only post bail for them, but also help them to get acquitted. She also points to an informal segregation within the Karachi central jail. A barrack has been set aside by the police and authorities for those known to be sex workers. When the authorities identify a young person among the sex workers, there is an assumption that she ought to be "saved" from sex work. Needless to say, the authorities do not provide substantive alternative life choices for those women who are so saved. Sabiha, aged twelve, was one such young girl. She was screened out of the barracks reserved for sex workers and put into a barrack for "regular" prisoners charged under zina. Unlike other inmates of her barrack, however, her bail was posted within two months of her incarceration, and she left the prison shortly after I met her. Another sex worker, Ghazala, aged sixteen, who had also been screened into the barracks for regulars, has no such connections. She had been in prison for one and a half years.

> I was in a hotel with a man. I have been to hotels with men before. My mother is sick, and my father is dead. I charge twenty-five rupees for zina. The first time I was fifteen. When my father died, we had a lot of debt, and creditors would come to our house and threaten us. Ami [her mother] said don't prostitute yourself. But I don't know where else to get the money so the creditors will not bother us. A friend of mine also does zina for money, and she showed me how to get clients. The man I was with is in jail as well. We were eating in a hotel, and the police caught us. My mother has come to visit me in jail, and she is trying to get bail money. But we have no money.

Ghazala's poverty, lack of education, lack of alternative options to earn a living, and lack of bail money are some of the reasons why she was in jail. She is not alone. Most women are illiterate and do not have the financial resources to post bail. In a sense, the zina laws are used to sweep clean the streets of women, particularly those who are poor, unwanted, and rebellious. Moreover, they serve to consolidate familial control over women's sexuality.

The laws are supposed to censure women and men for having sex outside of marriage, but, unlike Sabiha and Ghazala, who are sex workers, there is little conclusive proof that the women in jail had engaged in such sex in the first place. Many of them were merely accused of aiding and abetting abductions. A report by the Commission of Inquiry on the Status of Women (CIW 1997) suggests that the police have used the pretext of investigating zina to break into homes. They have arrested and locked up married couples for having illicit relations, widows for being suspect, and wives and daughters for not sufficiently complying with their families' wishes.

The police, as agents of the state, are delegated to protect the rights of citizens against violence. Yet frequently, it is the police who become perpetrators of violence. Women running from family control and coercion find the police to be another violent and corrupt adversary. At the hands of the police, they face sexual, physical, and emotional violence and extortion. Impoverished women have nothing with which to buy their way out of these situations, and they are the ones who suffer the most. The state's treatment of the zina victims calls into question the nation's commitment to protect the interests of all its citizens. Women are born into a national symbolic order that treats them as chattels to be bartered. The nation needs morality, and women and lower-class citizens are sacrificed to provide a moral face for the nation.

Women's narratives reveal gross misuse of the zina laws. Women who behave in ways that the men in their families do not like, often by choosing whom they will marry or divorce, are often accused of zina. Women who, for no apparent reason, incur the wrath of the men to whom they are married, even friends of women who want to leave their families or their husbands, are often charged and incarcerated under the terms of the zina laws. Women's male codefendants also suffer, but men often benefit from the bias in the laws that favours them. Zubaida, aged thirty-five, like many other women similarly situated, was accused of zina offences as a means of intimidating a relative – in this case, her husband – who is wanted by the authorities.

> My husband Nawaz repaired bicycles in a shop. One day the shop was robbed, and everyone thought he did it. They said he broke into the shop and stole a bicycle and some tools. The police suspected him, and he was afraid of what they would do to him. Everyone knows that if the police identify you as a thief, they beat you, and sometimes they beat you so much you die. Then they say the person had a heart attack or something like that.
>
> Well, Nawaz was afraid of all this happening to him; he came and told me that he was afraid and that he was going away for a while. I don't know where he went; I don't know where he is now. My children do not know where he is now. The police came and charged us under zina. Now my children and I are in jail.

Zubaida's account suggests that the police are using her and her four children as bait, in the hope that Nawaz will turn himself in or at least attempt to see his family. Zubaida had received no news of her husband during the past two and a half years that she had spent in jail, except for a letter in which he asked her to trust him and to trust in Allah. He would come for them, he wrote, when he could prove his innocence and when he had bail money to secure their release.

Many of the women with whom I spoke are impoverished and illiterate, and it is likely that they have not participated in the Pakistani political process. They do not vote, nor do they hold the state accountable when their constitutional rights are violated. Nearly invisible as citizens, they become even more invisible once behind bars. The women are not skilled workers and cannot make significant employment-related contributions to their family incomes. Hence their sexuality is used to generate wealth for the family. Fatima, aged fifty-one, could not provide adequate income for her family's needs. She begged in order to pay for food and rent but did not bring in enough money to support her husband's drug addiction. He suggested that she prostitute herself and charged her with zina when she refused.

A related aspect of this struggle is the relationship between the private sphere and the state. Myron Weiner and Ali Banuazizi (1994) identify a commonly held belief in Pakistan: there is an innocent and virtuous private sphere in need of protection from the state. The narratives of women whom I interviewed disrupt the binary between the state (public) and the family (private) and identify the contradictory forces that oppress and support women. At times, the state is a willing partner in families' desires to control their women. At other times, the state rules against the families and provides a place of refuge for women either in prison or in state-endorsed darul amans.

Resisting the Zina Ordinance

Zina laws do not wreak havoc in Pakistan without resistance. Women who are victims of the laws are contesting control of their sexuality and morality and, indeed, commodification of their bodies, particularly those women at the darul amans, where, despite the restrictive and oppressive conditions, many have *chosen* to find refuge. They are running away and seeking shelter from the domination and violence of fathers, husbands, brothers, and at times mothers who beat them and sell them in marriages to the highest bidders. They are choosing their own marriage partners, knowing that their choices place them at considerable risk. Despite the tremendous odds that they face, many of the women are rejecting their families' claims as they try to take control of their lives. Gulbaden Bibi, aged seventeen, described the struggles she is up against.

> My father sold me in marriage for 20,000 rupees when I was fifteen to Akram, who is fifty years old and a *zamidar* [landlord]. He used to beat me and yell at me and call me names. So my father helped me to obtain a divorce and paid back the 20,000 to Akram. Then I married my cousin, and father consented. Father drinks alcohol and gambles and takes opium and has a lot of debt. So he now wants me to divorce my cousin and marry a man in Karachi, who is willing to pay for me. This way father can pay off his debt. I refused. I want to stay with my husband, Qamar. Father said that there is no marriage between my cousin and myself, as I no longer have his permission to be married to Qamar. So he charged me with zina. I want to stay married to Qamar. I came to [the] darul aman voluntarily. I was afraid of what my father would do to me.

Married at fifteen and charged with zina at seventeen, Gulbaden Bibi had never been to school or voted in an election. She feared her father and had no support from her mother because, she claimed, "my mother is also afraid of my father; he beats her. [Moreover,] I do not want to end up like my mother." Her resistance to her family's attempts to control her is a political act. She had been in the Karachi central jail for eleven months when I interviewed her in 1999. The discursive practices surrounding zina identify Gulbaden as a participant in illicit sex. Prison has become a site of her moral regulation, while zina laws were one of the instruments used to put here there. Although the state is not the only agent of Gulbaden's regulation, the state provides a mechanism in the Zina Ordinance by which her family can control her. So, in effect, the state colludes in the process of pressuring rebellious Gulbaden to return to her family's fold.

Although the state invokes Islam as a rationale for zina laws, the women's narratives articulate that it is not religion but the collusion of familial control and state practices that is responsible for their plight. In rejecting the laws and the system that spawned them, the women also embrace the spirituality associated with religion. Thus religion becomes important even to rebellious women. They frame their resistance in religious terms, many invoking the mercy of Allah or resigning themselves to the will of Allah as they turn to religion to make sense of their situations. In turn, many become recruits for the Islamist group Women Aid Trust (WAT), which has been involved in rehabilitation work in the jails. Along with some NGOs, such as the Pakistan Women Lawyers Association (PAWLA) and Lawyers for Human Rights and Legal Aid

(LHRLA), WAT also helps women with their material needs. As Pakistan struggles to imagine its future, the moral regulation of poor women through zina laws serves to symbolically cleanse the material impurity of the nation.

The women with whom I spoke resist the attempts to control them, yet many also articulated a desire to be *gharaloo* (domestic) and *sharif* (honest), suggesting that they have rearticulated the middle-class ideal of domesticated, chaste, and honest women from a working-class perspective. Their families also want this of them. The women's narratives, however, indicate difficulties in maintaining domesticity, chastity, and honesty in their conditions of poverty. Combined with youth, this aura of domesticity and chastity commands a price on the marriage market, and many parents are loath to let go of such a valuable commodity without some kind of return.

For many women, zina is operationalized in ways that connect the process to monetary exchanges, highlighting the material predicaments of their families and suggesting that their economic situation is driving them to take recourse in repressive zina laws. Moreover, it leads us to speculate that control of morality and sexuality through zina might be used as a façade for material sustenance. What would happen if we did away with the zina laws; would the women still suffer? The violence that women face is rooted in social and political attitudes, with religion being used as an ideology that pressures women to accept particular norms. These norms were regulated through community censure. However, communities are not as integrated and under the control of kin groups as were in the past. Many of the women fleeing their families, it appears, can be regulated in towns and cities only through zina charges. This leads many to speculate that the women who actually commit zina are murdered in honour killings. Those charged with zina are "innocent" women,[9] and the families know that they are innocent. The primary purpose of these charges is to bring them into line with family wishes. The women's comments substantiated these commonly held beliefs. Many of their families, they recounted, indicated that they would post bail on the women's behalf and help to secure their release if the women initiated charges of abduction against their husbands and complied with family wishes. The women stated that they were in jail because they had refused, leading me to speculate that there are likely thousands who took up these offers of "help." We know only of those who resist and are in prison or have found refuge in the darul amans. In such places of formal and informal confinement, resisters negotiate a better bargain with patriarchy. They frequently take advantage of the literacy and skill development programs available to them. These patriarchal bargains open up new arenas of struggle and negotiation.

I want to draw attention to women's agency. Their narratives are a testimony to their poverty and to their endurance in the face of tremendous odds. However, those without resources are also frequently without social and legal assistance. The Islamist organizations and the NGOs provide these invaluable services, although not enough to help all the women. These organizations include WAT, Shirkat Gah, LHRLA, PAWLA, and the legal-aid cell AGHS, connected to the private watchdog organization the Human Rights Commission of Pakistan (HRCP). These agencies have successfully lobbied on the women's behalf and posed legal challenges to the laws, with the result that the government has brought fewer charges than in the past and that the courts have shown greater leniency to those charged with zina. In the next section, I begin with a discussion of women's status in Pakistan, before looking at ways that the Zina Ordinance is challenged.

5
Current Challenges to the Zina Ordinance

Status of Women in Pakistan

Pakistan has made considerable progress since 1947 as measured by several key social indicators, such as health and education. For example, between 1990 and 2003 life expectancy increased from fifty-nine to sixty-four years. Infant and maternal mortality rates have also dropped. However, significant gender disparities remain, particularly in education. On average, boys complete five years of school, while girls average only two and a half years. The rate of school enrolment for boys is 82 percent, higher than that of girls, which is 61 percent (CIA 2001). In 1998 only 3 percent of females between the ages of seventeen and twenty-three had access to higher education. In rural areas this discrimination against the girl child is more severe. In parts of Sindh or Baluchistan, the female literacy rates are 2 percent or less (USDS 2001). According to a *Statement on Gender in Pakistan* by the United Nations Development Program (2001), the country ranks 120th out of 146 countries in gender-related development and 92nd in gender empowerment. These gender indicators suggest that Pakistani women's lives and the decisions that they make continue to be affected by a lack of skill-based employment capable of providing them with a living wage.

Although the Constitution of Pakistan forbids discrimination on the basis of sex, women's legal status also remains ambiguous. There are several reasons for this. One is the male bias in the Pakistani legal system and judiciary (Bari 2002; Zia 1994), a bias present in other countries as well (Comack 2000b; Faith 1993). Recall that the Pakistani Constitutions of 1962 and 1973 require all laws to conform with the Qur'an and the Sunna. Furthermore, they suggest that a council on Islamic ideology oversee this process. Shahla Zia (1997) argues that this requirement has opened the door to formulations of law that draw on male-biased readings of the sacred and produce a status for women unequal to that of men. Moreover, the Zina Ordinance under which women have been charged and incarcerated was "recommended by the all-male Council of Islamic Ideology, passed by a heavily male-dominated assembly and interpreted by an all-male Federal *Shariat* Court. As such [it] reflect[s] the interests of the orthodoxy and their insensitivity to gender concerns" (Zia 1997, 79). This subordinate status for women intensified in 1985 when the Objectives Resolution was made part of the Constitution, an addition that diminished women's constitutional rights.[1] Indeed, the women's narratives presented earlier in this book attest to their diminished status as a consequence of existing laws and accompanying institutional procedures. The double message of full versus diminished rights as citizens has resulted in contradictory court rulings. Some judges, Sardar Ali (2000) argues, do not afford women full rights as citizens. Instead, they give unequal status to women, justifying their decisions based on commonly used Islamic interpretations. Other judges favour the equality enshrined in Article 25 of the Constitution of Pakistan. The Zina Ordinance further strengthened the hand of the former.

Effects of the Zina Ordinance

The Zina Ordinance has also affected the construction and regulation of normal and deviant sexualities for Pakistanis, particularly women. Farzana Bari (2002) notes that, with the exception of two instances where men were awarded hadd punishments of stoning to death for illicit sexual activity, it has been women who have been so sentenced. These punishments were not carried out, however, due to national and international pressure. Because both men and women are needed for the "crime" of heterosexual zina,[2] the disparity in the sentencing of women as compared to that of men speaks to the deep gender bias in the law and to the larger social system within which it operates. Few statistics exist on how many women have been jailed and for how long since the laws took effect in 1979.[3] Opponents of the laws, however, argue their case based on conclusions drawn from limited studies and from the number of women in prison at any one time.[4] They claim that thousands of women have been charged and jailed under the ordinance for zina "offences" (Toor 1997; Rouse 1998; Saigol 1997; Shaheed 1997b; Jahangir and Jilani 1988). A newsletter published by the Human Rights Commission of Pakistan states that between 40 and 50 percent of female prisoners in jail are there because of the zina laws. Data for the period 1994-96, collected from the Women's Police Station in Karachi, suggest higher numbers, with zina-related charges accounting for as many as 80 percent of the registered cases (CIW 1997). Although many of the prisoners are released after trial, they face years of incarceration before trial. A recent study (HRCP 1997) of prisoners in Pakistan revealed that only 16 percent of women prisoners had been tried and convicted. Moreover, in the "lockup" before their transfer to prison women were vulnerable to increased instances of custodial rape and other forms of physical, emotional, and sexual torture (HRCP 1997). So much so that the Benazir government passed a law in 1998 prohibiting women from spending a night in a lockup. Instead, she is sent directly to jail. Comments by Hina Jilani (1998) suggest that nationality and citizenship do not influence these rates. Women from Bangladesh are also charged and imprisoned under Pakistan's zina laws. Many Bengali women are forcibly taken to Pakistan by human traffickers, often via India, for the purpose of domestic or sexual servitude. My data suggest that christian families also use these Islamic laws to control their daughters.[5]

The poorly paid police in Pakistan are known for their corrupt practices. At their hands, women face sexual, physical, and emotional violence and extortion both when their families implicate them for zina crimes and when, as prisoners, they accompany guards to their court appearances. Impoverished women have nothing with which to buy their way out of their situation, and they are the ones who suffer the most. The women with whom I spoke in prison have few resources with which to mount a legal defence or to post bail. Even if they did have the resources, bail has to be posted by a male: their fathers, brothers, or husbands. Often these men are responsible for women's imprisonment. Many of the women whom I interviewed believed that they were in jail because they had gone against their family's wishes. They had little knowledge of the law or of the legal process, knowledge that might eventually set them free. They relied largely on the legal-aid system for guidance and support, a system that Zia Awan (2000) points out is woefully inadequate. Islamization policies have not sought out and imprisoned impoverished women, but they, as the most vulnerable members of society, are the ones most affected by these policies (HRCP 1997). That the state has not put any energy into dismantling General Zia-ul-Haq's Islamization edicts suggests that their antiwoman legacy is not incompatible with current visions of women's role in society.

These practices suggest that, although Pakistani women's rights and guarantees of safety are enshrined in the Constitution, the larger society provides few safeguards for women against brutality and violence both in the public and private sphere. While participation in the public sphere by elite and middle-class women has increased in Pakistan, Weiss

(2001) notes that the family remains a place where women of all classes are denied full rights as adults. It is true that families frequently provide women with safety in the confines of the home, a private context where the state is not always able to guarantee their security.[6] This protection, however, comes with a price. Many women are encouraged to submit to family demands regarding their education, employment, and marriage choices, demands that are largely based on traditions within each family. Although traditions affect both male and female children, they are applied more vigorously to females. While many women find families to be a safe haven in a cruel world, other women experience violence, brutality, and exploitation within their families. However, many families are now in transition and living as transients in the shanty towns of large cities, where they are away from the control of kin networks. As more and more women have taken up paid work outside the home, their mobility has increased, if only to and from work. At the same time, they continue to be socialized as ideal daughters, mothers, and wives whose sexuality is under the control of more powerful members of their families. I argue that most young women acquiesce to these demands. However, the women whom I interviewed had rebelled against family wishes and had chosen their own life partners. Women's rebellion against family demands and their consequent incarceration for zina offences suggest that women are also contesting established boundaries within the family.

Rouse (1997) has identified the need for virtue and respectability for reasons of status and for protection against societal violence. Women with whom I spoke posed their challenges in the name of their religious rights. The space set aside as a prayer area within the prison was a very popular place with the women, and members of my discussion group at the Karachi central jail frequently came to the meetings with their rosaries in hand. In so doing, they restated their submission to religion as they claimed virtue for themselves as respectable and pious women.

Organizing Resistance against the Zina Ordinance

The women that I interviewed for this study who had been affected by the Zina Ordinance are largely urban lower-middle-class and working-class women. However, professional upper-class women have frequently organized resistance against the ordinance and have provided services through nongovernmental organizations (NGOs) that they have founded. These women are the daughters and granddaughters of women who participated in the struggle for Pakistan from colonial Britain. The older generation of activists approached women's rights from a perspective of social welfare and charity as well as from a perspective of human rights, their major achievement being the Family Ordinance of 1961.[7] The subsequent generation, which fuels the current women's movement, appears to be more interested in a feminist perspective that examines the patriarchal codes underlying the social and political system in Pakistan.

Although the Hadood Ordinances contribute to Pakistani women's subordinate status, the ramifications of the ordinances, particularly those due to the zina laws' antiwoman bias, were not anticipated by civil society, and they remained unchallenged for several years (Shaheed and Mumtaz 1987). Scholars (Weiss 2001; Shaheed and Mumtaz 1987; Gardezi 1997) argue that it was the 1981 Fehmida and Allah Bux case that solidified women's opposition to Islamization. Two years after the Zina Ordinance was decreed, Fehmida and Allah Bux, who had married against the wishes of the former's parents, were sentenced for zina. Bux was married already and the marriage to Fehmida made her a second wife. The parents successfully argued through the lower courts that since they disapproved of this marriage, it was null and void and that their daughter had committed zina with a married man. Thus, as a married man, Bux was to die by stoning, while Fehmida, as a single woman, was to be given one hundred lashes.[8]

Many women were outraged by this sentence, and those involved with Shirkat Gah, a women's advocacy group and research centre, called a meeting of all women's organizations. Lala Rukh Khan (2003) points out that as there were very few women's groups in Pakistan at the time, individual women were also invited. The initial meeting was attended by about thirty women, who resolved to organize a forum where women could bring their issues for debate and develop strategies for action. This meeting initiated the birth of Women's Action Forum (WAF).

WAF developed as an advocacy group that systematically raises women's issues at the national level and is not aligned to any political party. It provides a platform that brings together individual women and women's organizations. The women's movement did not begin with WAF, but it consolidated and became more focused with the regular incidence of collective action by women (Gardezi 1997). Moreover, sharing information among women resulted in a higher level of awareness of women's issues. Lala Rukh Khan (2003), a founding member, points out that WAF brought together all kinds of women, both believers and nonbelievers. Although these diverse positions were all examined from a feminist perspective, Khan states that WAF did not openly declare its feminist leanings. Its members feared that doing so might alienate large numbers of women from supporting it. Moreover, it was never clear whether WAF was a lobby and pressure group or a grassroots mass women's organization. Although some members pressured WAF to become a mass organization, its limited human and financial resources made this venture difficult, if not impossible. At the same time, other members, who were not always aware of the complexities of grassroots organizing, critiqued WAF for not being feminist enough.

Moreover, Shaheed and Mumtaz (1987) point to a division in perspectives within WAF. How should they frame their challenges to the state, within an Islamic or a human rights perspective? WAF Karachi primarily took a human rights perspective and worked on social issues that were not limited to gender. Members of WAF Lahore, Rawalpindi/Islamabad, and Peshawar, on the other hand, have views similar to those of Pakistani jurist Khalid Ishaq.[9] They believe that, in order to be relevant to large numbers of Pakistanis, challenges to the Zina Ordinance have to be conducted within an Islamic framework. Shaheed and Mumtaz identify two considerations that led the Lahore chapter to examine women's rights in the Qur'an as a way to challenge the antiwoman laws. The first consideration came out of the religious justifications used to sanctify the antiwoman laws. The women felt that it was important to expose these laws as having no basis in Islam. They believed that they could mount a stronger challenge if they based it on religiously defined parameters.

Recall that religion has played an important role in nation building in Pakistan; the second consideration stems from this connection. For many Pakistanis, religion and nationalism have intertwined to produce a national identity. Thus many women in WAF Lahore felt that a religious discrediting of the laws would have an enormous impact on their legitimacy in the minds of Pakistanis. However, these views are challenged by Fauzia Gardezi (1997). She argues against a response from the women's movement that is framed by religion. Gardezi believes that such a response expends considerable energy debating what Islam does or does not say and detracts attention from women's day-to-day problems, such as poverty and violence. Moreover, Gardezi is critical of the position of some WAF activists who have refused to identify themselves as feminists in order to generate more broadly based support from Pakistani women. Nancy Cook (2001, 38) supports Gardezi's position: "By nesting feminist demands in Islamic justifications, feminists risk fundamentalist control of their movement." Gardezi and Cook reiterate the commonly-held feminist position that women's empowerment does not need religious sanction. However, Ziba Mir-Hosseini (1999, 6) is critical of feminists who argue that it is irrelevant and dangerous to engage with Islam. She argues that muslim women's lives "are negotiated within changing cultural constructs, produced in response to lived realities, through debates that are now going on all over the [m]uslim world, through the voices of women and men who want either to retain or change the present situation." At the same time Mir-Hosseini (1999, 6, 7) emphasizes the importance of feminism for muslim women. She notes that: "it is important to locate women's demands in a political context that is not isolated from the women's movements and experiences elsewhere in the world. Feminism is part of twentieth-century politics, and only through participation in this global feminist politics can [m]uslim women benefit from it and its agenda."

Mir-Hosseini (1999, 277) provides examples from contemporary Iran, where, she states, religious authorities made women's concerns a central issue. At the same time, women's organizations and journals are engaging with religion for dialogue and change within the framework of Islam, thereby opening "up a space for the notion of women's social and human rights." Her comment that "Islam and feminism are not incompatible" (7) finds resonance in Amina Jamal's work (2005), who claims in her writing on Jamat women in Pakistan that "feminist projects must contend with Jamat women's discursive strategies in invoking a gendered subject that is deeply marked by religion/culture but nevertheless claims for itself the rights of universal citizenship from the modernizing nation-state." Jamal argues that Jamat women repeatedly invoke their status as muslim women as they claim their citizenship rights within an Islamic state. Although they claim a suspicion of feminism, their rhetoric as well as their political activities align the strategies of Jamat women with those of secular feminists in muslim societies, who, like some members of WAF, draw on feminist interpretations of the sacred to legitimize their demands. Such debates on religious versus secular rights remind us that the women's movement in Pakistan is multifaceted and can pose challenges to patriarchy on many fronts.

The debates within the Pakistan women's movement gesture to a larger debate within Islamic communities between those who advocate literalism and seek guidance for all things from religious texts and those who promote a more humanist agenda that takes into account international law and how it might be applied in muslim societies. The literalists see these latter positions as modern, Western, and anti-Islamic. However, as Islamic scholars point out, humanism has a long history in Islamic philosophy. The writings of twelfth-century Andalusian philosopher Ibn-Rushd (who was an early advocate of women's equality) and eleventh-century Iranian philosopher Ibn-Sina predate the influence of

Western colonialism on muslim societies and point to this history.[10] Nevertheless, this is a very contentious debate in Pakistan, one that helps to discredit the women's movement as Western-inspired and largely irrelevant to Pakistanis.

WAF, too, has frequently been affected by this debate and deemed irrelevant by many Pakistanis, some of whom also accuse it of being elitist and of articulating a Western-inspired feminism.[11] Although WAF does not have widespread support, its policies and initiatives have impacted Pakistani society in several important ways. It has pioneered coordination and mobilization of various feminist organizations and other progressive groups. These initiatives have allowed the "woman question" to be raised nationally at an unprecedented level through the efforts not only of women's groups, but also of groups not totally devoted to women's issues. Furthermore, WAF continues to provide resources with which to challenge antiwoman laws, policies, and practices. Successful challenges to state practices have created social, political, and legal precedents while helping individual women to secure just decisions. These challenges have also created an awareness of women's issues. Shaheed and Mumtaz (1987) note that, despite the existence of feminist groups and other progressive groups active in 1979, the Hadood Ordinances were passed without protest. Today, with the increased consciousness in Pakistan of women's issues, this is no longer possible. The women's movement is stronger and more active now than in the past when the ordinances were first proclaimed by General Zia. Any such move by the government to curtail women's rights would generate considerable controversy and debate. While WAF has largely been active in urban areas and was at the forefront of the struggle for women's rights in the 1980s, in recent times other groups have also emerged. These include the Sindhiani Tehrik, a rural-based women's movement associated with the political party Awami Tehrik. Sindhiani Tehrik has reached many women in the smaller towns and villages.

Current Debates: Supporters and Challengers

General Zia-ul-Haq, the architect of the Zina Ordinance, was killed in 1989 when a bomb exploded in the airplane carrying him and other senior army personnel. However, his legacy of Islamization in the form of policies and ordinances remains. It continues to provide a symbolic moral direction for an increasingly indebted and impoverished nation, where inflation rates and unemployment remain high. Although progressive groups, including those linked to the women's movement, have lobbied for the repeal of the Hadood Ordinances, little broadly based resistance has developed. Sadia Toor (1997) attributes this to the fact that not all Pakistanis are affected by these laws or view them as oppressive. Amanullah Malik (1998), a lecturer at the Law College of Punjab University in Lahore, for example, continues to believe that the zina laws, as part of Islamization policies, help to create a moral and just Pakistani society. Most of the women jailed for zina, he points out, are prostitutes. My investigation, on the other hand, suggests that the few sex workers who are apprehended for zina are released shortly after because of their influential connections. The principal of the same college, Professor C.M. Hanif (1998), also supports these laws. He argues that "the problem is not with the laws themselves but with the system and [that] the few miscarriages of justice occur because of the implementation of the law." Professor Hanif is critical of those people who oppose the law and is particularly opposed to Asma Jahangir, the chair of the Human Rights Commission of Pakistan. Hanif calls Jahangir an "agent of the West." Malik claims that women are in prison with just cause, while Hanif cites misapplication of a just law as reason for their plight. Both men also identify police corruption as another cause of suffering under the zina laws. Yet the analysis offered by both men stops short of acknowledging that women, particularly poor women, are the main victims of the Zina Ordinance – Hanif because he believes that there are only a "few" of them and Malik because he insists that they are "prostitutes."

The Jamat-i-Islami also continues to support the laws. However, comments made by Sabiha Razi (2001), president of WAT, the women's division of the Jamat, suggest that support for the laws is not firm. Razi's work with imprisoned women has led her to doubt the merits of the law. On the one hand, she voiced the party line and claimed that the Zina Ordinance, as an Islamic law, helps to ensure that Pakistan remains a moral society. On the other hand, she pointed out that some members of the Jamat support a reexamination of the Zina Ordinance. Razi indicated that the Jamat has asked the government to initiate a national debate on the laws. In order to prepare for this debate, the Jamat has begun a consultative process in the hopes of proposing legal reform. The process includes deliberations among religious scholars acceptable to the Jamat, Razi claimed. She did not think that feminist scholars, activists, or other human rights groups such as LRHLA and HRCP would be invited to participate in this process. Razi noted that because this is a religion-based law, members of the Jamat do not believe that human rights organizations have the required religious credentials to participate in this debate. Pakistani society is deeply contested, with secularists, modernists, and religious organizations all wanting to promote their vision for state policy and practices. Razi's comments suggest, however, that Islamists are likely not open to input or alliances with other stakeholders. In fact, members of Pakistani NGOs shared with me their concerns that religious organizations were not willing to work in collaboration with those whom they consider secular. How this issue resolves itself, given the growing visibility of religious influence in Pakistan, will no doubt shape social justice struggles in the future. Indeed, challenges to the Hadood Ordinances have coincided with their continuous review by the Council of Islamic Ideology, the constitutionally mandated oversight body that reviews all laws to determine whether they are in accordance with Islam. The reports outlining the council's discussions or conclusions are consistently unavailable, however.

It appears that material reality contradicts policy in Pakistan. State law includes a rhetorical commitment to general abstract principles of equality. Moreover, as a signatory to the Convention on the Elimination of All Forms of Discrimination Against Women (CEDAW), Pakistan has reinforced this commitment. However, state policies and practices legislate and enforce a diminished status for impoverished women. A moral and just society – the rhetorical goal of the laws – would undoubtedly be welcomed in Pakistan, as it would be in other places. The zina laws do not bring about such a society in Pakistan. Instead, the state oversees the regulation of discriminatory practices and reinvigorates a disciplinary culture harmful to the interests of women, particularly lower-class women.

The English-language press in Pakistan has frequently debated the idea that the zina laws – indeed, the entire set of prohibitions that make up the Hadood Ordinances – are contributing to social and political injustice. Many of these debates present accounts of individual lives as case studies with a focus on human rights. These human rights debates are largely absent in the Urdu, Sindhi, Punjabi, and Pushto papers. Instead, women's stories are sensationalized as human-interest stories. Rehana Hakim (1999), senior editor of the English-language magazine *Newsline,* points out that the people most affected by these laws frequently speak these languages. They are unlikely to follow the debates in the English-language press. Few of them can read and write, and if they are literate, it is in their local languages. The inability of those affected by the laws to mount a substantial defence, then, is due not only to their lack of resources, but also to their lack of awareness about the reach of the Zina Ordinance and about their rights under the law. In making this statement, I do not intend to imply that people who read and write English are not affected by these laws. Instead, I want to emphasize how class functions to divide those who can and cannot afford an English education.

The lack of awareness among women charged with zina is quite alarming. A survey conducted in 1988 found that 90 percent of the over ninety prisoners interviewed in two prisons in the Punjab were unaware of the law under which they had been imprisoned. Over 60 percent of these prisoners received no legal assistance (Jahangir and Jilani 1988, 134-36). A more recent report by Amnesty International (2002) suggests that little has changed since 1988. Moreover, comments made by Najma Parveen (1999), appointed in 1997 as the first female superintendent in a Pakistani prison, suggest that this lack of awareness is not confined to illiterate and impoverished people. Parveen, a former librarian, became aware of the implications of the zina laws only when she became superintendent and realized that over 50 percent of the prisoners in her charge were in jail for alleged zina violations.

Changing Visions, Changing Prospects

Recall that the military regime of General Zia-ul-Haq brought in the zina laws in 1979 to bolster its political base through alliances with right-wing religious parties. According to Pakistani jurist Khalid Ishaq (1999), the Zina Ordinance was meant to change the corrupt political system and help to bring about a moral and just Islamic society. However, Ishaq realizes that this has not happened. The laws have not changed the corrupt practices of the state. Rather, they have served to exacerbate these practices. But repealing them, Ishaq claims, would encourage a backlash from the orthodox, who generally support it. Although the religious groups have traditionally not had electoral power in Pakistan, it is generally believed that they have had the ability to generate street power in the form of demonstrations and general strikes. Only with the 2003 elections, and only at the provincial level, did the rhetoric of religious parties translate into electoral power (Raza 2003).[12] There are no statistics that indicate what percentage of the population endorse the laws. Ishaq's sentiments are supported by the fact that neither the Nawaz Sharif nor the Benazir Bhutto regime repealed the laws, despite the latter's statements against them when she was opposition leader. These were minority regimes, however, with little room to manoeuvre in any clear direction. Their lack of political power was exacerbated by the Eighth Amendment, in effect until 1997, which gave the Pakistani president power to dismiss an elected prime minister. Indeed, the president used the Eighth Amendment to dismiss the democratically elected regimes of both Benazir Bhutto and Nawaz Sharif.

Although the Bhutto and Sharif regimes did not appear to be as clearly aligned with pro-Islamic forces as those under the Zia government, policies toward women remained uncertain and daily violations of women's rights continued without adequate state response (HRCP 1997). All of these regimes have enjoyed Western financial and political support. In the West few questions have been raised concerning the misuse of religion or lack of human rights in Pakistan. The United States, in particular, has seldom used its influence with Pakistani regimes to press for an end to human rights violations.

It is generally believed that Zia was a religiously minded man who also used religion for political purposes. His devotion encouraged him to take advantage of pro-mujahideen pressures from the United States and Saudi Arabia and to promote the jihad agenda of Islamic radicals in refugee camps in Pakistan wishing to wage war in Afghanistan. In Zia's time, Pakistan was a front-line state in fighting what many states, including the United States and Saudi Arabia, considered the communist "threat" from the Soviets and their allies in Afghanistan. Islamization was a material effect of his vision. Zia's legacy of Islamization continues to haunt the existing Pakistani regime, another military dictatorship.

In marked contrast to Zia's vision is that of General Pervez Musharraf, the current military ruler of Pakistan. Musharraf presents himself as a secularist and a modernist, identifying Turkish modernist leader Mustapha Kamal as his hero. He rules Pakistan in a different world from that in which Zia promoted Islamization. Musharraf's world is still reeling from the effects of 11 September 2001. The pressures on his regime are also very different. The Soviets have withdrawn from Afghanistan, the pro-communist regime in Kabul has fallen, and the Cold War is over. The United States and Saudi Arabia no longer want to support or finance jihad in Afghanistan or any other place. In fact, the jihadis have become the new enemy. While Zia was encouraged by the United States and Saudi Arabia to strengthen the Islamic radicals, Musharraf has been pressured by the same forces to move against the same Islamic radicals in Pakistan and those who want to use Pakistan as a base for spreading jihad around the world. As General Musharraf moves against radical Islam, he still has to deal with General Zia's legacy, which includes the Hadood Ordinances as well as the influence of radical Islam in the army.

Although the Hadood Ordinances remain in force, the Musharraf regime has made some attempts to change policies and practices that are discriminatory. These attempts have generated considerable resistance. For instance, Musharraf recently backed a proposal to reconsider the controversial blasphemy law. Under this law, anyone can be imprisoned once accused of blasphemy by members of the public. Charges could be laid, for instance, for taking the Prophet's name in vain or for desecrating the Qur'an. Often minority religious group members, such as christians, are charged under this law, thus substantiating the claim that the blasphemy law results in their facing further discrimination and harassment. Musharraf's proposed amendment states that a case can be registered under this law only if the district administration has first investigated the veracity of the matter. In other words, unsubstantiated accusations will no longer lead to arrest and imprisonment until trial. This is only a procedural change, as it does not change the effects of the law where there is ample evidence to prove that blasphemy has indeed occurred. The proposed changes, however, could potentially deter people from making false accusations. The Islamic parties rigorously opposed this modest change, and on 20 May 2000 Musharraf backed down. This exchange suggests that even an unelected military dictator, who has no responsibility to a potential electorate, cannot do whatever he likes. Musharraf is vulnerable to the Islamic parties for several reasons. First of all, Zia's legacy still permeates the Pakistan army, the strongest political player in the country. Also, the Islamic parties have made substantial political gains at the provincial level.

Although they appear unable to repeal Zia's discriminatory laws, comments made by members of the current regime suggest that they may be more willing than previous regimes to uphold human rights. Musharraf's inaugural address to the Convention on Human Rights and Human Dignity on 21 April 2002 in Islamabad provides an example. He stated, "It shall be the endeavour of my government to facilitate the creation of an environment in which every Pakistani can find an opportunity to lead his [*sic*] life with dignity and freedom" (AI 2002, 4). While it is true that virtually every ruler makes a commitment to uphold abstract principles of human justice and gender justice, the Musharraf regime has taken some steps in this direction. The country's National Assembly has been expanded to 350 seats, 60 of which were reserved for women (BBC 2002). Furthermore, a National Commission on the Status of Women was set up on 17 July 2000. Its mission includes an examination of laws related to women, with a view to identifying those that are discriminatory (AI 2002, 5). This mandate was echoed in a statement made by the minister of the interior: "All discriminatory laws against women should be repealed or amended to remove discrimination against women" (6).

Benazir Bhutto, too, attempted to enhance women's status. In 1994, when she was prime minister, the executive branch of the Pakistani government (the Senate) created a Commission of Inquiry for Women (CIW). Its terms of reference included a review of all existing laws that discriminate against women or affect their right to equal citizenship. The commission was mandated to amend existing laws and to bring them into accord with the values enshrined in the Qur'an and the Sunna.

Even though many commission members were not classified as "feminist activists," they reached a consensus on several critical points. The CIW report noted application and content problems in the Zina Ordinance. High incarceration rates along with low convictions of those charged with zina suggest widespread misuse of the ordinance. Moreover, the commissioners examined the laws from a perspective of religious scholarship and concluded that these laws did not conform to either Islam or the Pakistani Constitution and recommended that the Hadood Ordinances, including the Zina Ordinance, be repealed.[13] Despite these recommendations, the ordinances remain in effect.

Shaheen Sardar Ali, the minister responsible for the status of women under Musharraf's regime, called for another review of antiwoman laws. Moreover, Dr. Faqir Husain, secretary of the Law Commission of Pakistan, recently commented that the Hadood Ordinances are discriminatory and anti-Islamic, while the Council of Islamic Ideology decided, once again, to review the laws (*The Nation*, 2002a).

Making Political Sense of the Zina Ordinance

These initiatives suggest that the antiwoman laws passed during Zia's time are not supported by the current regime. Furthermore, the large acquittal rate of 95 percent demonstrates that, by and large, the judiciary does not find most zina charges valid. People in the prison system also want change. Najma Parveen was superintendent for women at the Karachi central jail when I interviewed her in 1999. She openly criticized the Zina Ordinance: "This law should go. It results in innocent women being imprisoned, and it takes away from resources that can be used for other prisoners. We don't have so much room in the prisons. Why are these women and their children here? I do not understand." Parveen called in a young boy, around eight years old, who was sweeping outside her office. "This boy was arrested along with his mother and grandmother and young sisters. They are all in jail because a neighbour ran away with her boyfriend and his family was implicated by her parents. Why is he here? Tell me what am I to do with him?"

Criticism from such diverse sections of society suggests that informed opinion is usually against the Zina Ordinance. Nevertheless, the material reality of women's lives in Pakistan remains largely unchanged. Budgets and five-year plans prioritize the military at the expense of poverty and development issues. Even under the democratically elected regimes of Nawaz Sharif and Benazir Bhutto, ordinary Pakistanis had difficulty accessing state services without bribing officials. Increasingly, Pakistani regimes have demonstrated a dismal human rights record. As for women's rights, few people in Pakistan would say that women do not have rights either under Islam or the Constitution. Yet, despite General Musharraf's assurances, the rights of women, particularly lower-class women, are systematically denied in political forums, institutional practice, and family traditions.

How do we account for the disparity between government intentions and its policies and practices? More to the point, why does the current political and military leadership lack the political will to bring about change? While there is no clear and definitive answer to these questions, I will nonetheless attempt to answer them by pointing to at least three interrelated phenomena. First, I want to identify the economic and political conditions that play a part in sustaining the Zina Ordinance. Second, I argue that national and international alliances between the military and religious groups maintain the status quo and appear to marginalize the rights of impoverished women, the most vulnerable members of society. Third, I want to point to the sanctity of laws deemed religious by large numbers of people.

The economic and political conditions that I identify are connected to the forces of globalization that have affected economies worldwide, causing the retrenchment of government services, particularly in third-world countries, such as health care, primary education, and state subsidies for essential goods (Chakravarthi 1990; Bello 2000). These structural adjustments are connected to access to international aid. They have helped to integrate economies of the South into North-dominated markets and have also increased poverty and violence in third-world societies (Bello 2000). Cultural devaluation of the third world, another significant factor, also stems from the colonial period and is reinforced by the new forms of colonialism linked to globalization. Many peoples in the third world face not only poverty, but also increasing devaluation of their traditions and ways of life. Dislocation due to urbanization also generates insecurities among the peoples of the South and exacerbates the situation. Economic and cultural crises lead even those regimes that define themselves as secular to identify religion as a significant organizing principle of society and to seek greater legitimacy through political alliances with religious forces in their regions. Iraq, after the Gulf War, is one such example. When Iraq's infrastructure was destroyed during the war, Saddam Hussein fostered alliances with Islamists and passed a series of antiwoman laws, including laws that focused on keeping women "moral." Gema Martin Munoz (1999, 10) argues that, "Whereas at one time the most pressing concern was to achieve modernization, now introducing morality into the political and socio-economic order has come to the fore as a result of the corruption and the marginalization that the state has generated." She claims that this desire for morality is connected to the reassertion of Islamic identity.

Such a scenario also exists in Pakistan, where reasserting an Islamic identity remains connected to nationalism in a context of recurring political and economic crises. Edited memories of past glory fuel the national imagination, while at the same time the general population are suffering the effects of globalization (Bennet Jones 2002; Talbot 1999). The national imagination, too, has begun to shift. As Aijaz Ahmed (2000) points out, both India and Bangladesh have larger muslim populations than Pakistan. The latter's reason for existence has begun to shift from being a homeland for muslims on the subcontinent to being the home of "pure muslims" in the region. The pure muslim, the one connected to the imperial past, a time when muslim aristocrats ruled much of the subcontinent, is an ideal largely attained by those Pakistanis who are male and propertied. Most Pakistanis, by virtue of their gender and class, have only a tenuous claim to this ideal. Interestingly, the largely "decadent" muslim aristocrats would not qualify as ideal candidates for current state prescriptions of morality. Yet this past is reimagined as a time of purity and power and violently forced on the nation; ordinary citizens are then sacrificed and regulated in the quest for purity. Decontextualized religious laws, including the zina laws, are often used as mechanisms of regulation.

There is another aspect of this process of regulation. Pakistan is a heavily indebted country, and it continues to borrow every year. Consequently, the priorities of the Pakistani government include making payments on the national debt and submitting to restructuring directives such as devaluing the rupee, raising the price of essential goods, and cutting back on infrastructure, including health care and education (Burki 2001). Additionally, the state has been committed to military spending due to its longstanding dispute with India over Kashmir (Schofield 2000). The Pakistani state also needs to keep multinational investors happy by providing a docile labour force. This means suppressing societal violence resulting from the rising price of basic foods and from high unemployment rates that are frequently connected to economic restructuring.

The state juggles these contradictory demands and maintains a delicate balance. Repealing the zina laws would threaten this balance. Pakistani nationalism is integrally connected to religion. The zina laws are seen as religious laws, and dispensing with them would pose a symbolic challenge to the nation. Their repeal has the potential to ignite a flame of protest within an unhappy and increasingly impoverished populace that has not been included in the benefits of globalization.

Recall that Zia's Islamization legacy has contributed fundamentally to the presence of radical Islamic groups in the Pakistan army. As the Pakistani state uses Islamic extremists to fight a proxy war in Kashmir, a close collaboration between the army and the extremists has strengthened this influence. Moreover, there has been a general refusal to reign in Islamic extremists and a perceived need to support anyone involved in the Kashmir struggle. Although Musharraf is trying to downplay the role of religion in the state, he has to deal with well-organized and well-armed Islamist militant groups. Profits from a very lucrative drug trade also influence these forces. According to a United States Department of State (2000) report, Afghanistan and Pakistan remain major suppliers of heroin in the world. Militant groups, together with state officials and international mafia, control this very lucrative drug trade. With large amounts of drug money at their disposal, radical Islamic groups are able to purchase arms on the open market, even if they do not get support from the Pakistani military. These groups are in a position to resist government changes to Zia's Islamization program and to mount substantial street protests. If Musharraf takes on the Islamists, it is widely believed that he will have to choose his issues carefully.

The United States' war on terrorism has been generally unpopular in Pakistan. Many Pakistanis have reacted negatively to American-led campaigns to oust the Taliban regime in Afghanistan and the Saddam Hussein regime in Iraq. There have been demonstrations on the streets, and Americans have been attacked; this opposition has been led largely by the Islamic parties. These incidents supported the popular belief that, if Pakistan continued to participate in the Bush-led war on terrorism and to clamp down on radical Islamic groups in the country, statewide protests would erupt. But this did not happen. Musharraf has to a large extent used heavy-handedness against those who disagreed with and protested against his policies. Several issues arise from this scenario. First, despite Musharraf's rhetoric about human rights, these tactics do not bode well for the future of democracy in Pakistan. Second, the extent to which Musharraf can use an army sympathetic to radical Islamic groups to crack down on those very groups is an interesting question. Third, given its rhetorical commitment to democracy, how long will the United States support a military regime that uses heavy-handed brutality against dissenters? Some respond to this question with "forever ... as long as it is in the United States' interests to do so." In any event, such issues, as long as they remain unresolved, contribute to a recipe for disaster.

Musharraf faces a bleak domestic situation. Men and women commit suicide because they cannot feed their families; the corrupt bribe their way out of illegal situations; less than 1 percent of Pakistanis pay taxes; and the poor cannot afford the law. There are few state-run social-welfare programs. Social services that do exist are provided by foreign-funded NGOs and by local charity organizations, some of which are religiously based. There are not enough schools for poor children. Even where schools exist, they are out of the financial reach of many Pakistanis. World Bank restructuring stipulations mandate that the government charge school fees. Although these fees are as little as 50 cents per month, they are a significant amount for impoverished people with large families. Many cannot pay the fees and may also need their children's labour for additional family income.

Madrassas (Islamic schools) are available for those parents who are willing to send their children to school but cannot afford to pay. In 2001 there were 7,000 to 8,000 madrassas in Pakistan attended by 600,000 to 700,000 students (Bennet Jones 2002, 32). Not only do madrassas not charge fees; they also provide students with free meals. However, the madrassa curriculum is very limited. Teachers instruct students to read and recite the Qur'an, and there is little instruction in basic literacy or skills development, leaving few employment options for graduates. As a result, Bennet Jones (2002) points out, graduates often join radical Islamic parties and become holy warriors. As part of the war on terror, Musharraf has called for changes in religious madrassas so that their curriculum mirrors that of state-run schools. There are several major problems with this proposal. Teacher salaries are low, and there is a teacher shortage, particularly in the rural areas. Where will Musharraf find qualified teachers to teach the new curriculum in the rural madrassas?

Rubina Saigol's (1997) comments add another dimension to this issue. She suggests that a change from religious madrassas to state-run schools will not radically alter what students are learning in school. She notes that beginning in Zia's time and increasingly since the passing of the Shariat Bill in 1991,[14] the curriculum in state schools has incorporated a significant amount of religious and military ideology. Saigol's comments indicate that both the madrassas and state schools promote religiosity and militancy among students. In order for Musharraf to address these issues, his regime will have to develop more comprehensive policies that link curriculum development to forms of employment not limited to religious militancy.

Challenging the madrassa system and withdrawing support for jihadis in Kashmir and elsewhere are two important issues that Musharraf has to deal with in a country where the 2002 election brought an increasing number of Islamists to power. These issues have the potential to generate enormous unrest and instability in the country. As a result of pressure from the United States, Musharraf did an about-turn in January 2002 regarding Pakistan's support for the Kashmiri insurgents. He banned two powerful jihadi organizations active in Kashmir, a move that resulted in domestic pressure from Islamic groups. Under American pressure to rein in the terrorist elements, Musharraf appears to have chosen to challenge Islamic parties over their support for worldwide jihad, particularly jihad in Kashmir, rather than to repeal of the antiwoman laws.[15]

Recently, the debate surrounding the Hadood Ordinances has resurfaced. There are calls from women's organizations and human rights groups as well as from prominent lawyers and jurists asking for a repeal of the ordinances. These views are opposed by the opposition groups that formed the Muttahida Majlis-e-Amal (MMA), a loose alliance of Islamic parties, which at the provincial level controls two of Pakistan's four provinces: North West Frontier Province and Balochistan (Raza 2003). With all these issues to consider, the Zina Ordinance might once again recede to the back burner, particularly since victims of zina laws are not considered an important political constituency. According to an elitist notion of enfranchisement, these people do not vote.

Middle-class ideas of elections often dismiss the needs of the "poor and illiterate." Such views deny that impoverished women can also determine their needs despite their lack of education. Such determinations render the human rights of zina victims a low priority within Pakistani regimes, particularly since they are usually released at trial anyway. There are many problems with this reasoning. First, even though the women are released upon trial, their lives are often destroyed as a result of their imprisonment. Second, the state cannot afford to provide adequate facilities for its prisoners within the jails or rehabilitation programs for them upon their release. Third, use of these laws by families helps to regulate the behaviour of vulnerable members of these families. Fourth, the laws provide yet another instrument with which to terrorize and extort money from an impoverished population. Fifth, the Zina Ordinance helps to exacerbate the general backlog in the Pakistani courts.

Sixth, the ordinance contributes to Pakistani society's general malaise, including continued gender injustice and violence against women. As such, the task of feminists who are organizing for change becomes that much harder.

The sanctity of religious laws is a third phenomenon which keeps the Zina Ordinance intact in Pakistan. Laws – or cultural practices for that matter – which politicians may reinforce to bolster various political agendas become in a sense sacred cows. However, once in place, it is not so easy to disavow them. For example, female genital mutilation is seen in some parts of Africa as a socio-religious practice. Discrediting or banning it has proved immensely problematic for both the state and for women's organizations. Similarly, the Zina Ordinance's connection to Islam, however slim it may be, frequently turns it into a cause to rally around and a hot issue for the state to tackle.

Issues Presently Confronting the Pakistani Women's Movement

Recent developments in the Pakistani women's movement need to be linked to the growth of the NGO phenomenon. In response to budget cuts stipulated by the World Bank and the International Monetary Fund, the state retreated from providing social structure and infrastructure for Pakistanis. As the state retrenched from these responsibilities, it became a mere enforcer of global rules at the local level. Resistance to these rules mainly comes from civil society, in particular, social activists, academics, and what are referred to as new converts to social justice within the establishment (Mallick 1998; Pasha 2001).

The women's movement, too, has been influenced by these trends. In more recent years, Lala Rukh Khan notes (2003), Western women's lobbying has resulted in greater international funding for women's programs in Pakistan.[16] More funding has enabled a larger number of programs to reach poor women at the same time that the women's movement has become more mainstream. I have found all kinds of women involved in providing services for women through NGOs who have little feminist politics. Also, many of the women who are beneficiaries of these programs cannot claim to be feminists either. Greater NGO funding has, however, impacted feminist activism. While in the 1980s women's activists lobbied for systemic change, Khan notes (2003) that this kind of activism, although still present to some extent in Bangladesh, has diminished in intensity in Pakistan, India, and Sri Lanka. Farzana Bari and Saba Gul Khattak (2001) refer to these trends as part of the "NGOization" of the women's movement. Women's agendas are co-opted through a process that funds "safe" issues such as women's health, education, and micro-enterprise. At the same time, women activists have little energy left to organize against gender-biased practices of the state.

As social activists in Pakistan point out, there is development money available for researching and providing services to women. There is little money, however, for infrastructures such as women's shelters as they do not fall under the category of "service provision." Therefore, while NGO legal-aid services are available to help women escape violent situations, there are few places to house and shelter these women once they have escaped. Dastak in Lahore and Panah in Karachi are two women's shelters run by feminist NGOs. There, women can find refuge while they explore their options. Their other alternative is to try to get shelter in one of the darul amans, where they are channelled into marriage or sent home to the family situations that they want to escape. Uzma Noorani of WAF claims that raising funds for women's shelters is one way that Western feminists can join forces with activists in Pakistan. They can raise funds privately and also put pressure on Western states and funding agencies both to increase funding and to change the rules so that funding shelters through foreign aid is permitted.

Although the NGOs provide invaluable resources and services, they also have their critics. Jacob Levich (2003) has challenged the view of NGOs as benign and progressive agents for change. Levich notes that NGOs played a crucial role in the 2003 coup that ousted the democratically elected leader of Georgia. He argues that United States funding to humanitarian agencies continues to be part of a strategy to build partnerships with local groups to bring about change that Washington desires. Levich (2003) quotes a USAID report, *Foreign Aid in the National Interest: Promoting Freedom, Security and Opportunity,* which maintains that American aid will no longer be used simply for development purposes, but also "to encourage democratic reform."[17] Levich argues that these words are frequently euphemisms for policies that are friendly to the United States. Indeed, his argument helps to identify NGOs as an arm of American imperialism. Although Levich's views are similar to the statements of Professor C.M. Hanif when he called a prominent Pakistani NGO lawyer an agent of the West,[18] they do not necessarily stem from the same political perspective. Levich is critical of American policies of exploitation and containment of progressive aspirations, while Hanif's comments suggest that he wants to promote a more Islamically oriented state in Pakistan and is critical of what he sees as interference from a secular West.

Yet another critique of NGOs suggests that the activists who work for them frame their resistance in terms of demands for women's human rights, which are a contested and controversial issue in the country. Pakistani jurist Khalid Ishaq (1999) argues that many of the challenges to the Zina Ordinance are largely ineffective because they continue to be exercised within a human rights framework, which supports a separation of religion and politics.[19] Debates generated by these challenges remain largely irrelevant to a conservative and religious general public.

Ishaq's views direct me to examine the ongoing debates about the uncritical uses of a human rights framework. Stemming from notions of humanity, human rights are considered inherent and inalienable (Dutt 1998). Social scientists have identified problems as well as possibilities inherent in this framework. For example, Grewal (1999b) suggests that the notion of human rights draws on a linear approach to development that sets up the West as a model for the rest of the world to emulate. Such an approach ensures the continuity and legitimacy of knowledge produced by the West about the non-West. Also, while human rights discourse asserts the rights of the individual, women are frequently not seen as individuals outside of the family group (Kothari and Sethi 1991). Notions of "women as a group" are problematic for those who critique metanarratives (such as those of universal human rights) and argue for a politics of difference (Weedon 1997). Others suggest that critiques of metanarratives should not be allowed to stop women from organizing and demanding their basic human rights (Baxi 1994). Moreover, Grewal (1999a) notes that recent calls to strengthen the links between trade and the human rights records of particular regimes have the potential to allow Western states to dictate what they define as human rights to the rest of the world. Despite the ways that minority and Aboriginal peoples are treated within first-world societies, such a link would no doubt reinforce the view that human rights is a third-world, not a first-world, issue. Grewal maintains that the current framing of human rights discourse cannot help us to understand the conditions of our lives. Instead, she makes a case for a vision that incorporates global economic and social justice.

Grewal's comments point to another problem with universal human rights discourse: not all subjects are conversant in it. Although many activists are versed in the discourse, large numbers of Pakistani citizens are unable to use the language in order to demand their citizenship rights. Certainly, narratives of women interviewed for this study suggest that the majority are able neither to secure help from the NGOs because of the overwhelming demands for their services nor to find a forum where they can articulate and demand their rights as human beings. Instead, many of the women with whom I spoke demanded justice through religious rights. "Allah has given us rights, and our families want to take them from us," one woman noted. It was a sentiment that many others had expressed.

Despite the dangers of an uncritical use of this framework, a call for women's human rights is also filled with possibilities. In keeping with the feminist slogan "the personal is political," a human rights framework propels the injustice that women suffer in the private sphere into the public one as a human rights issue. For example, the right to choose a marriage partner or to divorce a brutalizing husband is, many scholars believe, a muslim woman's inalienable religious right. However, in the private space of familial interactions and negotiations, women are often denied these rights. The large number of women who are charged and incarcerated for zina offences highlights this fact. In demanding these rights in the name of their humanity and/or religion, women enter political space as citizens. Such a process identifies a human rights framework as one of the few tools available to activists with which to fight fundamentalist state policies. Indeed, calls for social and economic justice for women have been posed in a human rights framework that demands government compliance with CEDAW. These conversations suggest a split between those forces that demand gender justice in the name of human rights and those that use interpretations of Islam to promote women's rights.

Though the promise of justice and equality for all embedded in human rights discourse has not been fulfilled, Grewal (1999a) notes that demand for human rights remains one of the few options for marginalized populations. At the same time, exploitation through transnational corporations and their local clients, who are frequently members of repressive regimes, continues. Many of these organizations and their local representatives use human rights language, which Grewal argues is frequently criticized for being ahistorical and apolitical. At the same time, interventions by some NGO activists frequently focus on local patriarchies and do not challenge the ways that international patriarchies support indigenous injustices. In effect, NGO activities and interventions often support the international status quo. For example, the legal-aid organizations that receive foreign funding, including from American foundations, do not challenge the United States government or the State Department for how their interference in Pakistani politics helped to create both the situation that brought in the Zina Ordinance and the conditions that continue to sustain it. Instead, they use their resources and energies to challenge the local state.

Although there is, I believe, valid criticism of the role that NGOs play in third-world societies, including Pakistan, I maintain that some of them, particularly the feminist NGOs, do act as powerful and progressive champions of people's rights. The activists who work for these social-welfare organizations often find themselves on a collision course with the state and law-enforcement agencies over civil and human rights issues. Their challenges nourish a climate where unjust state procedures and directives are questioned. These challenges are presented within a framework of human rights and progressive interpretations of Islam. The Nawaz Sharif regime felt threatened enough by such challenges that it tried to muzzle the media by imprisoning prominent journalists and harassing several prominent NGOs into being more supportive of government policies.

Although vulnerable to claims that they are Western agents and un-Islamic, foreign-funded NGOs are subtly changing Pakistani society (Mallick 1998). Many legal challenges to the Zina Ordinance have been raised by NGOs, such as Lawyers for Human Rights and Legal Aid and the Human Rights Commission of Pakistan. These challenges have occurred in conjunction with trends identified by a United States Department of State (2000, 46) report indicating that the Pakistani government is bringing fewer charges against women under the Zina Ordinance than in the past and that the courts are showing greater leniency toward women in sentencing and granting bail.

Narratives of women whom I interviewed suggest that their legal and religious rights have been violated and that this has happened largely because they are impoverished and because they are women. Their lives, when examined as embedded within local and international systems, provide a direction for feminist analyses that are neither Orientalist nor neglect the oppression of Pakistani women. Indeed, I believe that a transnational feminist analysis provides a strong framework both for examining how the local and global are connected to oppress women in Pakistan and for reconfiguring my own position as a native informant.

6
A Politics of Transnationality and Reconfigured Native Informing

Toward Transnational Feminist Solidarity

I now return to some central questions in this discussion: How can women challenging local and national patriarchies link up with, and draw support from, feminists internationally? In negotiating such transnational solidarity, what kinds of discourses and material relations are important to consider? What kinds of conversations would help to support transnational feminist solidarity? What issues surround a reading of the difficulties of third-world women's lives? What kinds of reconfigured native informing might support these processes?

I have maintained that the reception of analysis by third-world women as well as their activism does not take place in a vacuum. Instead, it occurs in a context of prevailing discourses and power relationships. Edward Said (1978) has identified these discourses as Orientalism and maintains that the Orientalist produces her identity through an articulation of difference from the other. Such articulations are particularly forceful, as I have argued elsewhere (Khan 2001a), in narratives of third-world women. They suggest that women living in Islamic societies are oppressed by the ways that the sacred influences state policies in fundamental ways. At the same time, an idea of a secular West where reason reigns supreme is commonly projected onto an equally monolithic sacred Islamic world as an ideal that the latter ought to emulate. Within such a framework, issues affecting women's lives are deemed the result of unchanging Islamic culture. This discussion contributes to an analysis that challenges such views. I have shown that the Zina Ordinance is not a product of an uncomplicated reading of an ahistorical sacred. It is very much a product of a very particular ongoing history that is both sacred and secular.

The woman charged with zina and incarcerated in a Pakistani jail is defined as deviant because of her uncontrolled sexuality and positioned to resist the control of her family and the power of the law. Why does she end up in prison? I have shown that it is not only because of religion. Instead, her poverty and illiteracy leave her more vulnerable to new forms of tradition circulating under the guise of religion. She is impoverished and illiterate not only because the state is spending less and less money on education and job creation, but also because her femaleness is commodified within a society structured by neocolonial injustices. As Pakistan continues to remain enmeshed in neocolonial exploitation, more and more women suffer the effects of poverty and violence. At the same time, state and familial control over their sexuality is consolidated.

Similar issues exist in the West, where feminists have long problematized the social construction of the impoverished and minority woman as deviant, as one whose sexuality needs to be controlled. As the state retrenches and provides fewer services, such as health care, basic education, and employment opportunities, women, particularly racialized poor women, become more vulnerable to conditions of poverty and violence in both the third and the first worlds. These issues are connected to patriarchy, capitalism, and new forms of control under globalization.

Such structural issues that link the local site in Pakistan to global relations are largely absent from conventional accounts about the zina victim and other issues that third-world women face. Instead, stories of third-world women serve to remind women living under Western patriarchy that they are better off than the woman whose genitals have been mutilated, or who is forced to veil, or who has to face the zina laws. The zina victim as spectacle stands for all Pakistani women, while the existence of the woman activist who fights for her release in Pakistan is totally denied. Such a scenario might help the Western woman to participate in the illusion that she is free and equal in her own society. In effect, the zina victim is rendered a metaphor for all that is wrong with the third world and by implication all that is right with the first world. Such an analysis frequently generates a desire in the West to save third-world women.

Sedef Arat-Koc's (2002) comments support my view. In her analysis of relations between first and third worlds, she notes that accounts by the former about the latter frequently generate rescues as part of a larger mission to civilize third-world peoples. Sensationalized accounts of zina victims would certainly reinforce the commonly held perception that muslim women are in need of rescuing. Although feminist analyses supporting such rescues of third-world women have been challenged in recent years (Mohanty 2003b; Min-ha 1989; Khan 2001a), such rescue attempts nevertheless frequently influence local perceptions of indigenous feminists in particular ways. These women are labelled "Westernized" – and, therefore, "undesirable" – and their efforts are undermined. Moreover, rescue efforts by first-world women also risk being co-opted by those with nonfeminist agendas in their own countries. The recent case made by George W. Bush's administration for saving Afghan women as a prelude to war in Afghanistan provides an example of such rescues. Should a future American administration be searching for a pretext to bomb Pakistan, the excesses surrounding the zina laws would certainly provide them with one. I have argued that such a process immobilizes many third-world women: Should we speak out against local patriarchies or not? Understanding how the local site is structured by the dictates of the larger structure of international relations provides a way out of such a potentially demobilizing dilemma. In this case, it means examining how international policies helped a dictator to proclaim the Zina Ordinance and how local as well as international pressures on Pakistan continue to sustain it. Moreover, Arat-Koc's recommendations that first-world women question the regressive policies in their home countries and how these policies help to sustain imperialism provides them with alternative actions to rescue missions. Such transnational feminist solidarity can help both first- and third-world women to identify the linkages between the local and the global and to challenge oppressive practices that sustain them. What form does transnational solidarity take? And how can such solidarity help in the struggle against the Zina Ordinance in Pakistan as well as against other antiwoman policies and practices? It is to an examination of these questions that I now turn.

Transnational Feminism

Inderpal Grewal and Caren Kaplan (1994) have made a persuasive case for a feminism that cuts across local and national boundaries and examines transnational linkages while challenging binaries between first and third world. An examination of international economics and politics as interlinked reminds us, they argue, that critiques of the nation-state are not sufficient to understand the injustices that continue within national boundaries. Understanding these transnational linkages helps us to determine that globalization colonizes lives and bodies and suggests that we utilize contextualized feminist projects to develop anti-capitalist strategies. Such linkages identify how "the local and global are simultaneously present in all contexts" (Dua and Trotz 2002, 76). Just as the forces of globalization are not limited to national borders, so, too, must forms of collective resistance be formulated at an international level. We cannot understand the past history and current politics sustaining the Zina Ordinance without looking outside the borders of the Pakistani state. Nor can we formulate effective resistance strategies.

Chandra Mohanty (2003a, 2) argues that such resistance calls for a feminism without borders, one that "acknowledges the fault lines, conflicts, differences, fears, and containment that borders represent. It acknowledges that there is no one sense of a border, that the lines between and through nations, races, classes, sexualities, religions, and disabilities are real – and that a feminism without borders must envision change and social justice work across these lines of demarcation and division." Mohanty's vision of feminism without borders is supported by Veronica Schild's (1999, 79) description of transnational feminist links as those "that disseminate resources, spinning ever-wider webs that entangle different women, who are nevertheless not some place outside of it." These webs are woven, she goes on to say, through a consistent translation, adaptation, resistance, and recoding of cultural symbols. Interlocking national and international power relations, particularly those connected to Cold War politics, helped to generate the Zina Ordinance. The American-led war on terrorism has replaced Cold War politics as a major influence on the policies of the region, policies that help to sustain the ordinance. Moreover, writing and reading about the current conflict has ramifications in the first world, where bashing Islam is on the rise. Feminist resistance must incorporate all of these issues if it is to be a transnational and multifaceted strategy for social justice.

A just and inclusive transnational feminism allows us to identify the workings of power and strategies of resistance at local, national, and global levels. It suggests transformative possibilities linking women across class, national, and racial divides. Not only does this transnational feminism connect the testimonies of imprisoned women in Pakistan to my search for identity in Canada, it also allows women at diverse national and local sites to engage in solidarity action and demand justice.

Women's conferences sponsored by the United Nations (UN), including those at Mexico City, Rio de Janeiro, Vienna, Nairobi, and Beijing, have allowed feminists to strengthen transnational networks that have helped to forge this solidarity.[1] Sonia Alvarez (2000) maintains that the Beijing preparatory process, in particular, further reinforced the international solidarity exchanges initiated in the 1980s and 1990s. These exchanges not only facilitated the development of connections at the organizational level, but also helped to forge personal links that gave women's groups a more vocal presence in national politics.

Some scholars do not fully endorse the process initiated by the UN-sponsored conferences. Nighat Said Khan (2002) points to a paradox. On the one hand, the women's movement has arrived in the corridors of power and is recognized by the United Nations as an active player in international politics. On the other hand, there is an intensification of the North-South divide, including more insensitivity from white women in the North. Said Khan identifies a binary in the statements made by many of the Northern women present at the Bejing + 5 Conference, a binary that reasserts a duality between the West and Islam and that does not fully understand the diversity of muslim societies or the connection of many current forms of Islamic fundamentalisms to United States foreign policy. She argues that to some extent the women's movement has been mainstreamed, its agenda co-opted and depoliticized. Many of the programs endorsed by feminists within large aid agencies, such as the Canadian International Development Agency (CIDA), focus on gender-neutral issues and deny the specificity of women's oppression. Moreover, Said Khan claims that the rhetoric of democracy and human rights is the new ideological strategy for dominating the world. These human rights are narrowly defined in economic terms focusing on the rights of consumers to make choices about the products that they buy. What is increasingly left out of this process is the human right to have food, shelter, clothing, education, employment, and freedom from violence.

Amrita Basu's (2000, 72) comments caution us against treating "international conferences as synonymous with transnational women's movements." Although she argues that the two have grown simultaneously, the women's movements are larger than the UN-sponsored conferences and include nongovernmental organizations (NGOs), social movements, and issue-based projects and campaigns. Many large Northern funding organizations that are committed to strengthening civil society, including the Ford Foundation and CIDA, have identified women's organizations as key players in this venture. The reliance of Southern-based NGOs on financial support from Northern foundations and institutions not only diminishes radical social-change projects, but also leaves them susceptible to charges that they are a mouthpiece of Western imperialism. Basu argues that the latter charge is not always valid. Despite foreign funding, many of these organizations define their own goals and objectives. For example, transnational networks like Women Living Under Muslim Laws (WLUML) and Development Alternatives with Women for a New Era (DAWN) are organized by and for women from the South. The effectiveness of transnational women's organizations is uneven, however. They are most effective when advancing women's civil and political rights and least effective when demanding freedom from poverty. Regardless of their shortcomings, women's organizations initiate and support North-South and South-South conversations. Such conversations accompany strategies for resisting injustice and strengthen women's agency. At the same time, they initiate important networks and alliances. What do some of these conversations look like?

North-South Conversations

North-South conversations identify interaction and strategies of resistance between first- and third-world feminists. Often these very diverse women have to deal with cultural and linguistic barriers. Conversations that challenge these barriers and move us away from the binary between the first and third worlds also allow us to examine, for example, how antiwoman practices manifest themselves in different locales. Simultaneously, they identify the ways that policies of first-world countries can and do affect women's lives in third-world societies. Naila Kabeer's (1999) research with Bangladeshi garment workers in Bangladesh and in England allows us to examine the transnational parameters of international trade. She claims that international standards must be devised that recognize how forces of inclusion and exclusion operate in local markets. Failure to do so, Kabeer argues, would work to the benefit of dominant forces in international trade and further marginalize women. Informed by such an analysis, first-world women's strategies of resistance can move beyond rescue work to target their own politicians who support these unfair trade policies. At the same time, they can imagine ways that transnational solidarity and resistance with third-world women can be forged. Indeed, recent successful campaigns against the labour practices of Nike and GAP in third-world countries revealed the extent to which first- as well as third-world feminists and other activists can exert power on these organizations internationally.

The Safia Bibi case and its resolution provide another example of the workings of North-South transnational solidarity in a zina case. Eighteen-year-old Safia Bibi, a virtually blind girl from Sahiwal, Pakistan, was a domestic servant in the home of a local landlord. She was raped by him as well as by his son. Safia became pregnant as a result of these rapes and gave birth to a child who later died, whereupon her father registered a case of rape against the perpetrators. Since there was not enough evidence to prove these rapes under the Zina Ordinance (four male muslims who had witnessed the act of rape), the two men were acquitted. Safia's accusation of rape and subsequent pregnancy, however, became a confession of her guilt of extramarital sex, for the judge ruled that she had committed zina. However, because of her young age and near blindness, he maintained that he was giving her a "light" sentence, which consisted of a public lashing (fifteen lashes), three years' imprisonment, and a fine of 1,000 rupees. Members of the feminist organization Women's Action Forum (WAF) were outraged by the verdict and publicized the case. Nationally, the coordinated activities of women's organizations and other progressive groups coalesced into an effective lobbying campaign that presented joint statements against the ruling to the state. Internationally, various feminist organizations raised the awareness of the issue to the extent that Pakistan's ambassador in England was questioned by reporters (Shaheed and Mumtaz 1987). He, in turn, wired Pakistan asking for an answer, prompting General Zia-ul-Haq himself to intervene in the case. Due to this pressure, both national and international, the case against Safia Bibi was brought back before the Federal Shariat Court, where it was subsequently dropped.

The Feminist Majority (FM) and its challenges to UNICOL Corporation's proposed operations in prewar Afghanistan also provide examples of transnational solidarity. Prior to 11 September 2001, UNICOL was negotiating with the Taliban regime in Kabul to install a pipeline across Afghanistan that would allow Central Asian oil to flow to the Caspian Sea. The Feminist Majority responded to requests from Afghan feminist groups, including the Revolutionary Association of Women of Afghanistan (RAWA), operating in refugee camps in Iran and Pakistan as well as in the United States, who feared that the $100 million that the Taliban stood to gain from the project would help to entrench their power in the region. The FM successfully lobbied Congress and UNICOL to the extent that UNICOL cited pressure from the Feminist Majority in its decision to abandon the project.[2]

Despite it successes on behalf of Afghan women, Arat-Koc's (2002) comments about rescue becomes relevant for the FM's challenges to the Taliban. The ambiguous position of many feminists from the North on the American-led war to "rescue" Afghan women from the Taliban endorses the military policies of the Bush regime and is an example of an uncritical global sisterhood. Such a sisterhood, Arat-Koc claims, does not challenge the regressive political developments in the first world, yet it provides legitimacy and support to new forms of imperialism in the guise of rescues. She endorses a feminism that recognizes the co-option of human rights and women's rights rhetoric for new military agendas, and she advocates an engaged feminism. Such a feminism goes beyond a narrow focus on women's issues to "engaging with an array of issues from foreign policy, to immigration, to civil liberties, to sovereignty" (63).

Arat-Koc's comments about an engaged feminism contribute to the successful workings of transnational solidarity, which, Sonia Alvarez (2000) maintains, not only draw attention to particular issues internationally, but also provide a sense of international community for feminists who may be facing uphill battles in their own locales. North-South conversations about the Zina Ordinance move us away from a focus on the "goodness or badness" of the laws and toward an examination of how international flows of power and capital have influenced patriarchal control of women in Pakistan. Moreover, these interactions position us to imagine and initiate collaborative projects that help to illuminate each other's oppression. While conversations between women from the North and the South are important in bringing about social change, another set of conversations is also crucial to building solidarity and to challenging oppression. These are the South-South conversations.

South-South Conversations

South-South conversations facilitate knowledge sharing and collaboration among countries of the global South. For example, my research suggests that in Pakistan women's sexuality is commodified and controlled through a complex process in which intersecting forces of religion, militarization, and globalization play a part. Women's sexuality in Thailand is also commodified as the country continues to serve as a haven for sex tourism. An analysis of the similarities and differences in such commodification of women's bodies across national borders allows for an examination of the ways that third-world women's sexuality contributes to international flows of capital and resources.

Such an analysis has helped to reconfigure prostitution, transforming it from a moral issue into a form of work that generates income. Notions of sex work then become aligned to labour that women and men do and allow for demands for decent and safe working conditions (Kempadoo 1998b). La Union Unica, a Mexican organization founded in 1993, provides an example. This association works with sex workers and with the businesses from which these workers operate to improve labour conditions for the sex workers. At the same time, the organization runs literacy classes for children of sex workers and operates a shelter for sexually abused and pregnant women. La Union Unica has also developed contacts with other sex-worker organizations in Brazil and Uruguay (Cabezas 1998). A call for safe working conditions generates AIDS-prevention health initiatives. The Synergy Women and Development Program (SYNFEV), founded in 1987 in Dakar, Senegal, seeks to address women's concerns regarding health, particularly sexual and reproductive health, as well as women's right to control their sexuality (Tandia 1998). Another important organization, the Centro de Orientación e Investigación Integral (COIN), developed in the Dominican Republic (Kempadoo 1998a) partly as a response to the spread of AIDS among the sex-worker population. COIN, whose activities include research and education through popular theatre, organized the first international congress on prostitution and sex work in 1995. International linkages allow women to learn from each other about the usefulness of strategies for resistance. Such knowledge and action allows for, as Arat-Koc (2002) suggests, solidarity based on unpacking the material and ideological underpinnings of oppressive practices. Moreover, initiatives based on such solidarity have allowed feminist visionaries to forge ahead with programs that take the movement beyond those proposed by the state.

Scholarship and activism generated by the international solidarity network Women Living Under Muslim Laws provides another example. As part of its Women and Shar'ia Law Project, WLUML brought together women from different muslim countries around the world. Together, they were able to generate discussion and ideas about how different versions of "authentic" muslim laws were being used to curtail women's rights in diverse contexts. The documents that they produced generated much discussion regarding not only the dissimilar ways that the laws affected women, but also the similar contours of how patriarchies at different locales draw on selected symbols of the sacred texts of Islam.

StreetNet, an organization of street vendors from countries in Latin America, Asia, and Africa is also an example of an organization that encourages South-South conversations between women's groups. Members of StreetNet note that street vending is increasing all over the world as a result of job losses and lack of employment in the formal economy to such an extent that this activity represents one-third of the urban workforce around the world. The majority of street vendors in most countries are women who seek the right to vend without harassment as well as access to selling spaces in locales that customers frequent. Moreover, they want storage and child-care facilities as well as basic infrastructure, such as water, shelter, and toilets. Conceived in 1995 by the International Alliance of Street Vendors, StreetNet aims to secure these rights and facilities.

The Self-Employed Women's Association (SEWA) is yet another organization through which women in the South exchange ideas and network across national borders. Founded in 1971, SEWA soon established itself as a trade union helping poor, self-employed women workers to earn a living through their labour or through small business ventures. SEWA organizes women workers for full employment so that they may obtain various forms of security, including health care, child care, and shelter. This association has chapters in India, South Africa, Yemen, Turkey, and Brazil and is at the nexus of three movements: the labour movement, the cooperative movement, and the women's movement.

North-South as well as South-South linkages have done much to enhance international solidarity among women. They encourage not only an analysis of women's lives as connected to local patriarchies, but also an examination of how international power relations influence these patriarchies. Such a process facilitates a transnational feminism that makes the global visible in the local and the local visible in the global. The United Nations Development Program (UNDP) has helped to encourage some of these movements. The UNDP position suggests that countries of the South are linked by history and geography as well as by the challenges that they face. They have important lessons to share, including some success stories. Although comments by Amrita Basu (2000) and Nighat Said Khan (2002) suggest that the interests of United Nations organizations and the transnational women's movement are not always aligned, the UNDP encourages cooperation between various organizations through a global knowledge network that includes 132 countries.

Such conversations help North-South as well as South-South organizations to develop transnational feminist networks and to forge international solidarity among women. In identifying the importance of conversations, it is not my intention to say that conversations alone will bring about solidarity or that they can change the unequal power relations between first- and third-world feminists. Instead, I want to identify the importance of conversations to forging solidarity and to imagining strategies for change that generate success stories from their ability to transcend borders. As transnational corporations and their effects on women's lives transcend borders, so, too, many theorists argue, should women's strategies for challenging these effects be transnational. What would such strategies and their challenges look like? A recent collection of essays by Nancy Naples and Manisha Desai (2002) provides some answers. The authors document the ways that women organize and challenge oppressive and exploitative global forces across first- and third-world divides. In effect, such transnational feminist practices identify the interlinked effects of globalization among local, national, and internal geographical spaces. For example, Yoko

Fukumura and Martha Matsouka (2002) argue that viable strategies for opposing militarization are suggested by the activism of Okinawa Women Act Against Military Violence (OWAAMV), which targets the gendered and environmental damage resulting from discrimination by the Japanese against ethnic Okinawans as well as from the presence of the United States military in Okinawa. Their challenges include documentation of sexual violence and of environmental damage off the coast of Okinawa. OWAAMV uses direct action against the United States military as well as against local and national authorities and makes presentations to international women's groups and environmental groups. Recognizing the need to build international pressure, OWAAMV organized peace caravans in the United States in 1995 and 1998. Moreover, members presented briefs to the US Congress. OWAAMV's campaigns, Fukumura and Matsuoka point out, have allowed them to develop and internationalize their leadership skills and to build a broadly based movement with international networks through information sharing and collective strategy. OWAAMV has created broad alliances and potential resources through its ability to network across "lines of class, nation and the division of urban and rural" (258).

The efforts of Central American Women in Solidarity with Maquila Workers (the Network) provide another example of progressive third-world organization (Mendez 2002). Consisting of women from Guatemala, Honduras, Nicaragua, and El Salvador, the Network was formed in 1996 and meets every six months in different countries. Its members realized that posing challenges at the local level was not enough; they also had to challenge the larger international relations that reinforced local oppression. Issues that they have taken up include exploitation of children in the export free zones (including the maquila factories), violence against women (including sexual violence), reproductive health, and sexism within unions. The Network documents the conditions in the maquila and shares strategies and information with other activist groups. They also collect information on transnational corporations and launch regional, national, and international campaigns to raise public awareness. Although they document the exploitative conditions prevalent within maquila factories, members of the Network do not call for the removal of maquila plants. Instead, they lobby for better conditions and better pay within maquila factories. To achieve its goals, the Network makes strategic use of local, regional, and international media to increase public awareness of issues of concern to maquila workers.

In an effort to bring about the demise of the Zina Ordinance, challenges from transnational feminist networks can help to formulate an analysis and politics that reinforce national pressure with pressure from international feminist organizations. Such challenges also discredit Orientalist notions that render invisible progressive forces within third-world societies. Feminist solidarity politics might also discredit Orientalist perceptions of muslim women as they question conventional accounts of the ways that stories are told and retold. Indeed, such transnational action would challenge the reductive opinions that my belligerent colleague articulated about muslims after the Chomsky lecture that we both attended (an incident discussed in the Introduction).

Such a politics brings us full circle, back to where this book began its discussion: native informing. It is imperative that feminists and other progressive groups begin to move away from an uncomplicated reliance on knowledge that the native informant imparts to the first-world researcher and audience. Instead, we must see accounts of the informant, the researcher, and the audience as coming out of particular histories and power relations. I recommend that we understand the analysis of the Zina Ordinance through a process that also examines narration and how it is read.

Reconfiguring Native Informing

Earlier in this discussion, I identified at least three native informants who help to narrate the Zina Ordinance and its effects: the woman who is charged with and confined for zina offences; the Pakistani activist who challenges the system and helps to secure her release; and myself, a Canadian academic originally from Pakistan who is producing an account largely for a Western audience. There is another person in this narrative as it travels across national and class borders. She or he is the reader who brings to the interpretation of my account her or his own history of compliance with and resistance against the dominant perspectives about women, the third-world, and Islam that permeate Western societies. Let me speak to each position.

The woman charged with zina speaks of her choice to rebel against familial authority and demands her rights in the name of religion and/or the law. Can she be seen as an agent capable of speaking her "truth"? Social theorists argue that experience is discursively produced and cannot be an unproblematic grounding for understanding our lives. For example, Joan Scott (1992) and Joanne Passaro (1997) have cautioned against a sole reliance on narratives of experience. Scott is concerned that there are many structural relations outside the experiences of the narrator, while Passaro believes that women might be "blamed" for their choices and consequently for the predicaments in which they find themselves.

Many of the women with whom I spoke had not been given a voice in family decisions around their marriages. They frequently suffered from exploitative demands imposed on them by their present and former husbands and by other family members. In their individual acts of rebellion, they had little personal and institutional support. They blamed their families and corrupt government officials for their plight. They had little knowledge, however, of the forces that had brought General Zia to power or of those that had encouraged his role in the Cold War conflict in Afghanistan, a role that allowed him to trample on human rights in Pakistan with little international censure. Nor did they appear to be aware of the role that globalization, militarization, or the war on terrorism had played in their imprisonment.

I am not accusing them of false consciousness. I am merely cautioning against using their stand-alone accounts as testimonies of oppression. For if we take their accounts at face value, local patriarchies are identified as the cause of their situation. However, a change in local patriarchs, from General Zia to General Pervez Musharraf has not led to a repeal of the Zina Ordinance, despite the latter's stated good intentions. Looking beyond the nation-state can afford us a broader understanding of the issue. As we connect women's stories to a larger trend toward continued militarization of third-world countries, including Pakistan, it becomes apparent that militarization benefits arms-selling nations. At the same time, it impoverishes indigenous populations, rendering women particularly vulnerable to male violence and other forms of exploitation. Impoverishment at the local level is also connected to rising religious fundamentalism. Transnational feminism not only provides a more complex understanding of women' plight; it also helps to develop a multifaceted response by targeting local as well as international players in this process.

The rise in religious fundamentalism certainly affects the second native informant, the woman activist. Structural-adjustment directives have accompanied a retrenchment of services provided by the state, a trend that is particularly evident within third-world societies. Many of these societies rely on foreign-funded NGOs to provide services such as health care and legal aid to increasingly impoverished populations. As the third-world activist draws upon Western funds provided to the NGO that employs her, she is suspect – partly because she is a feminist and wants to change the status quo, but also because her feminism, even when critical of Western imperialism, is seen as connected to it. As the woman activist struggles against the violence and sexism that zina victims face, she, too, risks sexism and violence for not toeing the line.

Her activism has accompanied a 95 percent acquittal rate for zina victims, yet her struggles are largely invisible in Western mainstream accounts that sensationalize narratives of zina victims. Her situation demands a feminist solidarity that not only North-South but also South-South conversations provide.

I also want to revisit my position as the third type of native informant. Situated at the intersection of race and gender, I am located in the first world but not of it. My contradictory location helps me to complicate the binary between the first and third worlds while working toward a transnational feminist analysis of the oppression of women in Pakistan that disrupts the cultural, racial, and colonial divisions associated with the East-West divide. My political work demonstrates my commitment to Pakistani women's issues. In this way, my activities not only benefit my academic career *over here,* but also make a tangible contribution to women's issues *over there.*

At the same time, I want to note that my political statements about the Zina Ordinance are compromised by the ways that I, too, am complicit in reproducing Orientalist imagery and facilitating rescue attempts of Pakistani women. Such accounts not only solidify prejudice, but also have other kinds of contradictory implications. The United States Immigration and Naturalization Service (INS) move toward granting women gender-based asylum provides an example. Through the process of providing testimony, third-world women, Grewal (1999a) argues, are frequently positioned to reinforce stereotypes of their communities within the legal system. At the same time, it is through such testimonies that women at risk are granted asylum. There is a similar process in Canada. Sherene Razack (1998) has spoken about the ways that the publication *Guidelines to the Immigration Act* enables the Immigration and Refugee Board to take gender into account during the course of refugee hearings. While the *Guidelines* acknowledge sexual violence and abuse as persecution, they tend to evoke pity, as they pathologize the societies to which the women belong. Instead, Razack suggests, we should ask why women flee their homes and what the North's responsibilities toward them are.

I, too, have been co-opted into this process. I have found myself in the position of expert witness in cases where women's families claim that their daughters are committing zina with the men to whom they are married and threaten them with violence and death. The women have fled to the United States or to Canada and have asked for gender-based asylum. I have written affidavits on their behalf, and the women have been granted asylum. The affidavit format does not allow me to connect the local conditions in Pakistan to the global nor to identify the ways that policies and practices of international powerbrokers have contributed to the conditions of women's lives. I know that if the women are not granted asylum, they will be killed by their relatives. So I speak about the inability and unwillingness of the state to protect them from the violence of their families, and the women are frequently granted asylum. My testimony reconfirms the judges, lawyers, and immigration officials as "saviours" of these women. I speak on their behalf, and I am complicit in their rescues and in reconfirming that Pakistanis, muslims, and third-world people are backward and need saving. The discourse that allows women to be rescued also reinforces Orientalist and imperialist imagery to such an extent that, even as the United States or Canada is deporting muslim and Pakistani men, these few women are being rescued.

Having acknowledged, once again, my complicity in the process of pathologizing third-world and muslim women and facilitating their rescues, I return to the issue of native informing. Unequal power relations help to sustain it, and until they cease to exist, native informing will remain a problem. While transnational feminists and other progressive movements continue to challenge social and gender injustice, I suggest that we deal with the practice of native informing using the next best option. We have different conversations about native informing with a view to reconfiguring the practices associated with it. In particular, we can challenge the politics of benevolence emerging from Euro-American societies as we link local injustices to national and international relations. Indeed, these reconfigured conversations about native informing allow us to understand the links between the local and the global on two levels: the conditions that exist at the local level in Pakistan and the global context that sustains these conditions.

When we connect local injustices to global power politics, certain kinds of transnational practices become visible. While the Pakistani state evokes an eternal Islam to justify prosecution for zina, women's stories identify particular local and national arrangements. These arrangements suggest that the promulgation and continuance of zina laws appear rooted in a particular economic and political expediency. Women are intimidated into becoming docile bodies and participating in unequal relations with their families, their husbands, and their employers. At the same time, the continuation of state practices that are associated with the zina laws renders the incarceration and detention of women natural and normal. Through the zina laws, the state lays the groundwork for new forms of "traditions" that can be used to control future generations of women both at home and at work.

Women are figured as the biological and cultural reproducers of the nation. As such, their sexuality is a valuable resource that is utilized to service their families and the nation. Should they decide to enter associations of romance and love, they frequently face the wrath of their families. In this refusal to submit to parental pressures and pressures of former husbands, many women find themselves incarcerated in prison or more informally confined in the darul amans. Paradoxically, the state assists families to intimidate the women at the same time that it helps the women to escape the grip of their families by providing them shelter in state-run institutions. During the course of their confinement, many women learn to be independent of their families and gain basic literacy and life-sustaining skills, such as embroidery and sewing; however, they are traumatized by the process. At the same time, regulation of women's sexuality helps to build a case for national morality on a basis of societal corruption and injustice. The state considers lower-class women expendable, and their liberty is sacrificed for the moral health of the nation. Increasingly, structural inequality and growing societal violence can then be explained away as a lack of individual morality, rendering the cost of globalization and military spending invisible – spending that benefits countries largely located in the industrial North.

There is another aspect of this scenario. Pakistan, literally the "land of the pure," is ironically a corrupt state. Symbolism surrounding the Zina Ordinance, however, allows a national narrative of purity and perfection to mask the material impurity of the nation. Classed and gendered citizens are sacrificed to symbolically (re)establish the purity of Pakistan. Impoverished women's incarceration suggests that unwanted and undesirable elements have been eliminated from the "pure" land. The immoral polluting woman is imprisoned to keep the family and the nation chaste. Her incarceration and subsequent invisibility, both behind prison walls and when she drops out of sight upon release, gesture to a perfection of the state. This absent woman, however, is still present. Through the controversies surrounding the debate on zina, she continuously reasserts her presence in the national narrative. However, an Orientalist reading of zina in the West, through which she is seen as a passive victim of Islam, threatens to render these controversies invisible. Denied a presence because of her gender and class in Pakistan, the zina victim also risks being made invisible in the West by the Orientalist gaze.

Through my investigation, I reinsert into this debate the social and political milieu that surrounds zina both *over here* and *over there*. I recommend that we think of individuals not just as members of national or familial groups, but also in relation to wider political and social connections. Pakistan is a highly indebted and increasingly impoverished nation. Conditions arising out of unemployment, poverty, and the lack of social-service infrastructure will continue to generate instability in Pakistan. Social, political, and economic uncertainty in the country will likely prevent the government from repealing any law that threatens the status quo. This is the dilemma of the Zina Ordinance and what eminent Pakistani jurist, Khalid Ishaq (1999), gestured to in his comment that "the state is stuck with these laws."

The forces of globalization help to sustain the zina laws in Pakistan. These same forces also influence the movement of diverse peoples into diasporic exile in the first world. Reconfigured native informing identifies common fronts for these seemingly diverse struggles. At the same time, transnational feminist solidarity disrupts binary thinking about divisions between the oppressive third-world woman and the liberated Western woman, allowing for an understanding of how oppressions operate globally. Such a perspective might help Western readers of my account to understand how they might be situated vis-à-vis the Zina Ordinance. For example, do they know what international policies their local politicians support? Do they know where their tax dollars are spent? Do they challenge the constant barrage of anti-Islamic and anti-third-world commentary emerging from the media and from everyday conversations? Answers to such questions help first- and third-world feminists to engage in solidarity struggles as they imagine and deploy crucial strategies for transformative change locally and internationally. At the same time, they work toward theories and practices of alliance formation across difference.

Framework for Challenging the Zina Ordinance

I now return to what I believe is an important question concerning the most appropriate framework within which to pose challenges to antiwoman laws within Pakistan. Will these challenges be posed within a human rights or a "progressive" Islamic framework? Indeed, this question reinstates a binary between the sacred and the secular and creates divisions among feminists.[3] It also divides feminists from those women belonging to religious groups who are working with victims of the Zina Ordinance.

Minoo Moallem (1999) has identified a perceived dichotomy between the pronouncements of religious fundamentalism and what she terms egalitarian feminism influenced by liberalism. She points out that both positions are similar in many ways. Both challenge not only the project of modernity with its links to a colonial past, but also the new colonial present. As they advance women's subjectivity, both repudiate separation of the public and private spheres while advocating transnationalism. But there are also differences between these two positions. Although both are concerned with the body as a bearer of culture, religion, values, and morality, fundamentalism regards this situation as natural and mandated by God, whereas feminism regards it is as socially produced and in need of change. Furthermore, Moallem claims that whereas egalitarian feminism emerged as "a subject position within the pervasive masculinism of liberal discourse and its paradigm of equality, Islamic fundamentalism opposes the assimilatory forces of modernity, modernization, and Westernization to claim cultural uniqueness and difference" (324). While fundamentalists prioritize morality over politics, feminists prioritize politics over morality. Nevertheless, Moallem goes on to claim that no position is either exclusively fundamentalist or feminist; instead, she identifies movements and actors that are hybrid varieties of the two and notes: "Many fundamentalist women have started to negotiate and renegotiate their place in society within fundamentalist discourse, by using mainstream feminist concepts and ideas such as patriarchy and male chauvinism. In the case of feminists, certain culturalist positions, by depending on a form of essentialized nurturing femininity associated with women's nature and the construction of a glorious matriarchal past, thereby import fundamentalist components into feminism" (324-25).

I, too, do not support a clear split between fundamentalist demands for gender justice and the demands of those who frame their challenges within a feminist framework. However, in conversations with women from religious organizations and feminist organizations, I found that this split exists. Fatima, a woman who works for WAT, commented that her organization had worked with a feminist NGO to organize a meeting around women's capacity building. Although the women who came to the meeting were largely there because of WAT's outreach, once the meeting began, she claimed, the feminist groups took over. "We brought the women, and they pushed us to the side; I will never work with them again." I found similar sentiments among the many feminists working with NGOs. They do not want to engage in any collaborative projects with religious women's groups. "We do not have the same ideas about women's agency or want to limit her to predetermined parameters," one activist claimed. This lack of conversation and coordination between various women's groups is disturbing in light of increasing religious influence in Pakistan, a trend that has accelerated since General

Zia's time. Feminists and religious women's groups need to find creative ways to work with all stakeholders as they demand justice for women. This is a crucial component for developing conditions that enhance women's agency.

This division between the secular and the sacred gestures to a politics of paralysis, which Simon Murden (2002) argues is found in many muslim societies. Recent years have witnessed the destruction of the left in many muslim societies, such as Afghanistan, Pakistan, and Indonesia, and the strengthening of the religious right, in part because of Cold War politics. Since former colonies gained political independence, political Islam has been the principal opposition in many countries. Gudrun's Kramer's (1997, 73) comments support Murden's view. In recent years, she notes, "a growing number of [m]uslims, including a good many Islamist activists, have called for pluralist democracy, or at least for some of its basic elements: the rule of law and the protection of human rights, political participation, government control and accountability." Kramer further contends that, increasingly, muslims are distinguishing between the rules of religious duties, which they believe to be unalterable, and the rules covering political, economic, and social life, where revision is possible. Murden endorses this view and suggests that the *shura* (muslim consultative process) has the potential to develop into a more democratic model. As this process of consultation continues and strengthens, it will no doubt help to consolidate challenges to antiwoman laws and practices in the future. The situation in Pakistan is somewhat different, for it presents us with a case of state-led Islamization and its after effects. In recent days, however, opposition to the military regime of General Musharraf and its participation in the United States' war on terror has come primarily from religious organizations. Although such opposition has targeted the authoritarian state, it has also shown a remarkably low tolerance for dissent within its own ranks.

Conclusion

Jeffery Weeks (1986, 12) believes that "the increasing politicization of sex in the past century offers new possibilities and consequently challenges: not just of moral control ... but [also] of political analysis, opposition and of change." In Pakistan the Zina Ordinance has helped to reinforce and politicize the connection between sex and morality. At the same time, my analysis suggests, competing interests create the conditions for sustaining the zina laws as well as possibilities for change. While women have equality with men under the Constitution, state policies surrounding the zina laws produce conditions through which women, particularly lower-class women, are rendered less equal than men. State and civil interests also promote the zina laws as Islamic or allow them as a matter of political expediency. At the same time, there are forces that oppose the laws and activists who support women in their struggles. These contradictory forces in society allow women to move out of the position of helpless victim and give them room to manoeuvre.

The commonly seen spectacle of the caged sexuality of the Pakistani woman is an Orientalist vision that identifies muslim patriarchy as the cause of her oppression. Its interrogation connects the zina laws and the patriarchal oppression that they generate not only to colonial images but also to imperialist strategies that keep third-world countries impoverished in a web of unjust relations. Transnational feminist analysis demystifies the spectacle of the woman condemned under the zina laws and argues that her situation is not solely a function of local patriarchies. Moreover, such an analysis identifies those factors that obscure the link between the woman *over here* and the woman *over there*. In this manner, we identify how the local and the global interconnect in our lives.

In moving away from examining gender and culture as the only bases of Pakistani women's subordination, a feminist response must also move toward exploring poverty, corruption, and illiteracy as important factors contributing to their situation. These issues can be linked to structural-adjustment directives imposed on third-world countries, including Pakistan, by the International Monetary Fund and the World Bank. These are the same structural-adjustment directives that are increasingly responsible for the loss of funding for shelters and for women's organizations in first-world countries, including Canada, where I live, work, and write. The voices of women incarcerated under the zina laws should be scripted over an analysis of the effects of globalization. Feminist collective strategies must continue to examine and to challenge how globalization affects women internationally. Moreover, feminist strategies must be cognizant not only of how women's subordination differs at diverse sites, but also of how it is similar.

In terms of the current capitalist structure within which Pakistan is embedded, market value determines why things are done. There is no market value in giving women the choice to make decisions about their lives or in repealing the zina laws. Within a transnational feminist approach, the lives of the victims of the zina laws are not considered expendable in the pursuit of globalization and militarization. Moreover, in bringing structural issues back into a discussion of individual morality, this analysis moves away from a cultural-relativist position to identify the effects of the capitalist system that help to create the conditions sustaining the zina laws. At the same time, it identifies how I, as a native informant, risk being implicated in reinforcing Orientalist views of muslims.

In making my concluding statements, I reaffirm Chandra Mohanty's (2003b) call for a feminist analysis that examines the local and global as existing simultaneously and as constitutive of each other. The Zina Ordinance and its local effects on impoverished women in Pakistan also need to be examined as connected to a more broadly based trend toward militarization of third-world countries. Militarization benefits Western arms-selling nations as it impoverishes third-world peoples. At the same time, it leaves women more vulnerable to violence and exploitation.

Such an analysis demands exchanges based on transnational solidarity and reinforces Arat-Koc's (2002) call for a more engaged feminism, one that redefines women's issues to include critiques of imperialism and a call for sustainability. Connecting the local and the global allows the woman in Canada who is in an abusive situation to recognize that the forces of globalization responsible for a lack of shelter space for her are likewise implicated in the conditions that help to imprison Pakistani women for zina offences. Both situations are associated with state retrenchment of basic services and its accompanying poverty. Transnational feminist solidarity based on an understanding of these differences and similarities suggests a redefined sisterhood through which, bell hooks (1997, 410) argues, women struggle to understand differences and to build "a community of interests, shared beliefs and goals around which to unite."

I conclude with the following thoughts: the zina laws do not remain unchallenged within Pakistani society. By complicating the positioning of the native informant both *over here* and *over there* and by calling for transnational feminist action, this discussion seeks to reinforce these challenges. Moreover, strategies to liberate Pakistani women from these oppressive laws need to incorporate strategies to liberate Pakistani society from unequal power relations in which Pakistan is positioned as subordinate. Through such analysis and accompanying action, the transnational feminist project is not limited to understanding women's place in the new world order but seeks to change the new world order itself. Such feminisms might benefit from a political dialogue between the women and men who read my account and the native informants whom I have identified in this discussion: the woman charged with zina offences, the activist who works to secure her release, the academic who writes about them, as well as the reader of such accounts. Such a dialogue would enhance the power of transnational feminisms and the possibilities available to them.

The women whom I interviewed are clear in their desire to control their bodies and opposed to those who lay claim to them. By seeking refuge in darul amans and by risking incarceration, they are asserting their agency even as these state-sponsored spaces attempt to neutralize their efforts. Transnational feminist social action can support these women in their struggles and support the struggles of other activists in Pakistan by imagining and promoting solidarity as a means to identify and challenge how the local and global are connected to produce systems of injustice in Pakistan and elsewhere.

I want to end with Nighat Said Khan's (2002) observation that, in order to move forward, the women's movement needs the support and active collaboration of women of the North. Said Khan is clear that she does not want white women of the North to lead this movement. Instead, she wants the women's movement in the North to be led by women from third-world communities. What specific and concrete actions might result from such a development? The answer to this question is something for future activists and researchers to imagine and bring to fruition.

Notes

Introduction: Locating the Issue

1 To minimize sensationalizing religious labels, I do not capitalize "muslim," "hindu," "christian," and so on.

2 The native informant is a person who translates his or her culture and language for anthropologists. The notion of native informing will be developed throughout this manuscript.

3 *Hazoor Baksh v. Federation of Pakistan*, PLD 1981 Federal Shariat Court 145.

4 Pakistan is the only country with such social and legal censures. Cultural and religious distaste for zina has been formalized into law in several countries, including Nigeria, Saudi Arabia, and Taliban-ruled Afghanistan.

Chapter 1: Native Informing on the Zina Ordinance

1 Orientalism is a complex notion identifying a discursive production of knowledge about the Orient that has material effects. Orientalist knowledge is produced not only by Western scholars, but also by third-world scholars situated within the Western academy. For a broader discussion of Orientalism, see Said (1978). As social scientists (Alloula 1986; Khan 2001a) point out, two Orientalist tropes frequently identify the muslim woman. She is either forced to veil or she is the half-naked harem girl whose unveiled body is on display.

2 For a discussion of Western knowledge production about sati and female genital mutilation, see Mani (1990, 35) and James (1998).

3 This process will be further discussed in Chapter 3 of this book.

4 This discussion is also examined in Chapter 6.

5 My analysis was published as the book *Muslim Women: Crafting a North American Identity* (Khan 2000).

6 The notion of feminist solidarity across borders and what it looks like will be developed more fully in Chapter 6.

Chapter 2: Contextualizing the Zina Ordinance

1 The Ottoman ruler of Turkey was the *calipha,* the symbolic head of the muslim world. After the defeat of Turkey in the First World War, Mustapha Kamal Pasha, the modernist leader of the Turks, formally abolished the Caliphate and declared Turkey a modern nation-state.

2 In recent years there has been an exception to this trend. The military regime of General Pervez Musharraf has had to work alongside the Muttahida Majlis-e-

Amal (MMA), a coalition of six Islamist parties that came to power in the Northwest Frontier province in the October 2002 elections.

3 The Jamat-i-Islami is not the only Islamic party in Pakistan. For a larger discussion of this topic, see Bennet Jones (2002). I have, however, chosen to examine some of the policies of the Jamat not only because it is the most organized Islamic party in the country, but also because of the party's central role in influencing the Zia regime during the period of Islamization when the Zina Ordinance was proclaimed.
4 *Sunnah* refers to the extensive body of literature that attempts to document the teachings of, and personal examples from, the life of the Prophet Mohammad.
5 Conventional wisdom suggests that sentiments of religious extremism exist in the army. It is not clear, however, to what extent they exist. Unable to discern the actual amount of religious influence currently present in the army, Owen Bennet Jones (2002) notes that Western defence attachés have taken to counting beards at army ceremonies. The current beard count places religious extremism at 15 percent.
6 In Chapter 5 I will examine the reasons why the Zina Ordinance is still in place in the post-Zia period, during which religious parties have a diminished influence on the affairs of the state.
7 I will speak about this resistance in Chapter 5.
8 See Lawrence (1987) and Mernissi (1992).

Chapter 3: Speaking to the Women

1 Having obtained their addresses, I tried to locate two women whose families had accepted them back. However, I was given the run around by their relatives, who were suspicious of me and of my motives.
2 Yasmin's statistics support those put forward by the Human Rights Commission of Pakistan (HRCP). See page 84.
3 The consent forms were the standard description of the project in English. I explained the forms to the women in Urdu, while my research assistant and prison officials explained them in the other languages that the women spoke. I told the women that I was going to speak to them about their lives and then write about our conversations.
4 I have used pseudonyms when speaking of women charged under or escaping relatives who want to prosecute them using the Zina Ordinance.
5 It was never made clear to me by authorities how and why some women were "ordered" to join the group.
6 Although there is considerable recent scholarship on how prison labour, particularly nonwhite labour, has facilitated profit making in privatized prisons, this has not happened in Pakistan as yet.
7 In their analysis of contemporary Iranian women's lives, Ziba Mir-Hosseini and Kim Longinotto (1998) note similar expressions of agency. Iranian women's demands in the divorce courts for dignity and freedom of choice are couched in religious terms.

Chapter 4: Disobedient Daughters, Errant Wives, and Others

1 One lakh is 100,000 rupees (approximately Cdn $2,000).
2 Sind and Punjab are two different provinces in Pakistan. Naheed's parents are conflating provincial regional groups and ethnicity, as is often done in Pakistan.

3 It is important to make a distinction between "dower" and "dowry." The former is a religion-based practice through which monies are paid by the husband to his new wife. The latter is based on custom and consists of the monies and other goods that are given to the bride by her parents to help to set her up in her new home. In recent years, "dowry" has come to include gifts to many of the groom's extended family as well.
4 There are five schools of sharia: Hanafi, Hanbali, Maliki, Shafi, and Jafferi. Hanafi law is commonly used in Pakistan.
5 *Humaira Mahmood v. State,* L1 *PLD* 494, Lahore High Court, 1999.
6 In a more recent court challenge, Humaira Mahmood raised these issues again, and the Pakistani woman's ability to contract marriage was revalidated through a unanimous court ruling in 1999. *Humaira Mahmood v. State,* L1 *PLD* 494, Lahore High Court, 1999.
7 See Amnesty International (2002).
8 Her bail could be around fifty thousand rupees. If she does not have cash, she can register property. The bail is to ensure that she does not run away (Yasmin 1998).
9 I do not make a distinction between licit and illicit sexuality. Therefore, I use the word "innocent" with some caution and point to the ways that the Zina Ordinance helps to reinforce a particular version of a chaste moral woman who is innocent of the charge of illicit sex and thereby distinguished from the woman who is not.

Chapter 5: Current Challenges to the Zina Ordinance

1 The Objectives Resolution has a curious history and has certainly affected women's rights in Pakistan. In 1949 various stakeholders prepared an Objectives Resolution with regard to the drafting of the Constitution of the new State of Pakistan. Religious parties, including the Jamat-i-Islami, were able to influence this process. The resolution, which declared that Pakistan would evolve into an Islamic state, was largely disregarded until the Zia regime made the resolution a part of the Constitution. As a result, the resolution helped to support patriarchal readings of Islamic religious texts, ensuring that laws passed in the name of Islam frequently granted women a subordinate status, thus undermining the equality granted them in the Constitution. In effect, as Shaheen Sardar Ali (2000) points out, with the Objectives Resolution now enshrined as Article 2a of the Pakistani Constitution, "one set of constitutional provisions are being used to undermine another set of provisions in the same document."
2 Interestingly, no statistics exist about homosexual zina perhaps because of a popular denial that there is any such thing as homosexuality in Pakistan. Where homosexuality does exist, it is perceived to be a Western import only practised among the Westernized affluent class.
3 The lack of statistics surrounding the application of the Zina Ordinance points to the larger unavailability of statistics concerning social problems. This shortage is partly a function of the lack of resources both at the state and NGO levels.
4 During my visit to the Karachi jail in December 1999, I was told that fifty of the seventy-six women in jail were there because of zina-related charges.
5 See Nausheen's comments on page 64.
6 I do not aim to identify Pakistan as the only place where the state is unable to guarantee women's safety outside the home. Instead, I want to point to the

increasing societal violence that is making both the public and private spheres unsafe for all Pakistanis, including women.

7 The Muslim Family Law Ordinance was passed in 1961 as a result of consistent pressure from women's organizations. It contained some advantageous provisions for women. For example, an effort was made to regulate the process of divorce, thereby restricting polygamy. The legal age of marriage for both males and females was raised. See Sardar Ali (2000).

8 This case mobilized women's groups and other activists, who fought on behalf of Fehmida and Allah Bux. The case went all the way to the Supreme Court, where it was finally dismissed.

9 See page 104.

10 See Malik (1999).

11 See Kishwar (1990) for a larger discussion of the debate about the relevancy of feminism for third-world women.

12 See page 101.

13 This is not the first women's commission to recommend changes to the antiwoman laws in Pakistan. Earlier recommendations had been made in 1955, 1976, and 1985. None of these recommendations were acted upon by the governments of the time.

14 The Shariat Bill was passed as a private members bill in 1990. It was part of a process designed to move Pakistan toward a theocracy. With a focus on the economy, the mass media, the judicial system, and education, it was an attempt by the religious right in the government to gain control of the legal and ideological machinery of the state. The Bill was vigorously opposed by the women's movement and other progressive forces in the country. It was also challenged by some of the religious forces who claimed it was not fully Islamic. In an attempt to strike a balance that would appease the religious right, the government passed a watered-down version of the Bill.

15 Kashmir, a muslim majority region, was ceded to India by its hindu ruler in a process approved by the outgoing British colonial administration. Pakistan challenged this event both diplomatically and militarily immediately after partition and has continued to do so. There have been three declared wars between India and Pakistan since 1947 as well as continuous conflict involving Pakistani and Indian army personnel, who fight each other supported by fighter jets. Pursuing policies of more indirect confrontation with India, Pakistan has supported radical Islamic groups operating in Kashmir. This support intensified in the recent ongoing insurgency against the Indian occupation of the Kashmir Valley, which began in the late 1980s.

Pressure from the United States was not the only reason that Musharraf withdrew his support for the jihadi groups operating in Kashmir. The Kashmir issue has hampered development for both India and Pakistan, with Pakistani military spending linked to that of India. While these policies divert significant resources to defence at the expense of poverty-reduction schemes, education, and health care in both countries, they affect Pakistan more than they do India. Pakistan's economy is much smaller than India's, and military spending affects Pakistan more than it does India. Gaurav Kampani and Haider Nizamani (2001) argue that, in its arms race with India, Pakistan is on a road to economic ruin. Musharraf appears to share this view, for in recent months he has unlinked Pakistan's defence spending from that of India and called for an end to reactive missile testing. These actions tested Musharraf's relationship with the radical religious elements in the country. Many of these elements want a strong Pakistani army that supports the insurgency in Kashmir and is ready to wage war with India.

16 This transnational women's solidarity work and its benefits to organizations in the third world will be discussed more fully in Chapter 6.

17 Many observers believe that USAID has always been used to advance American interests.

18 See page 91.

19 Ishaq served as a member of General Zia's Council of Islamic Ideology. Although he was present at the deliberations about the Hadood Ordinances, he voted against them, as he believed that they were ill-considered. Ishaq subsequently went on to oppose the laws in court.

Chapter 6: A Politics of Transnationality and Reconfigured Native Informing

1 For an examination of this process, see Alvarez 2000.

2 It is not my intention to unconditionally endorse the Feminist Majority perspective or to say that their analysis of the situation was without serious flaws. However, I do want to point to the ways that transnational feminist collective action can at times identify and successfully challenge injustice at diverse sites. See Khan (2001a).

3 This was discussed earlier. See pages 88-89.

References

Abu Loughad, Lila. 2002. "Do Muslim Women Really Need Saving." *American Anthropologist* 104, 3: 783-90.

Afkhami, Mahnaz. 1995. "Introduction." In *Faith and Freedom: Women's Human Rights in the Muslim World,* ed. Mahnaz Afkhami, 1-16. Syracuse, NY: Syracuse University Press.

Ahmed, Aijaz. 1983. "Democracy and Dictatorship." In *Pakistan, the Roots of Dictatorship: The Political Economy of a Praetorian State,* ed. Hassan Gardezi and Jamil Rashid, 94-172. London: Zed.

–. 1992. *In Theory: Classes, Nations, Literatures.* London: Verso.

–. 2000. *Lineages of the Present: Ideology and Politics in Contemporary South Asia.* London: Verso.

Ahmed, Feroz. 1999. *Ethnicity and Politics in Pakistan.* Karachi, Pakistan: Oxford University Press.

Ahmed, Leila. 1992. *Women and Gender in Islam: Historical Roots of a Modern Debate.* New Haven: Yale University Press.

Alam, S.M. Shamsul. 1998. "Women in the Era of Modernity and Islamic Fundamentalism: The Case of Taslima Nasrin of Bangladesh." *Signs: Journal of Women in Culture and Society* 23, 2: 429-62.

Ali, Abdullah Yusuf, ed. 1938. *The Holy Qur'an: Texts, Translations and Commentary.* Lahore, Pakistan: Sh. Muhammad Ashraf, Kashmiri Bazar.

–, ed. 1968. *Qur'an: Text, Translation and Commentary.* Beirut: Dar al-Arabia.

Ali, Tariq. 2002. *The Clash of Fundamentalisms: Crusades, Jihads, Modernity.* London: Verso.

Alloula, Malek. 1986. *The Colonial Harem.* Minneapolis, MN: University of Minnesota Press.

Alvarez, Sonia E. 2000. "Translating the Global: Effects of Transnational Organizing on Local Feminist Discourses and Practices in Latin America." In *Meridians: Feminism, Race, Transnationalism* 1, 1: 29-67.

Amnesty International (AI). 1995. "Foreign-Sponsored Human Rights Disaster Ignored by the World." AI Index, SAS 11/16/95, GMT 29 November.

–. 1999. "No One Here Sleeps Safely." AI Index, AMR 19/009/99.

–. 2002. "Pakistan: Insufficient Protection of Women." AI Index, ASS 33/006/2002.

Amos, Valerie, and Prathibha Parmar. 1984. "Challenging Imperial Feminism." *Feminist Review* 17 (Autumn): 3-19.

Anwar, Raja. 1988. *The Tragedy of Afghanistan: A First-Hand Account.* Trans. Khalid Hasan. London: Verso.

Anzaldua, Gloria. 1987. *Borderlands: The New Mestiza.* Reprint, San Francisco: Aunt Lute, 1999.

Appadurai, Arjun. 1996. "Disjuncture and Difference in the Global Cultural Economy." In *Modernity at Large: Cultural Dimensions of Globalization,* 27-47. Minneapolis, MN: University of Minnesota Press.

Arat-Koc, Sedef. 2002. "Imperial Wars or Benevolent Interventions? Reflections on 'Global Feminism' Post September 11th." *Atlantis* 26, 2 (Spring/Summer): 53-65.

Awan, Zia. 1999. Interview with Zia Awan, President of Lawyers for Human Rights, Karachi, Pakistan, December.

–. 2000. "The Status of Legal Aid in Pakistan." In *Human Rights Link: A Quarterly Newsletter,* D-1, 1st Floor, Court View Apartments, Opp. Sindh Assembly Building, Court Road, Karachi–74200, Pakistan.

Bannerji, Himani. 2000. *The Dark Side of the Nation: Essays on Multiculturalism, Nationalism and Gender.* Toronto: Canadian Scholars.

Bari, Farzana. 2002. "Tyranny of *Hadood* Laws in Pakistan." *The News* (Karachi), 17 May.

–, and Saba Gul Khattak. 2001. "Power Configurations in Public and Private Arenas: The Women's Movement's Response." In *Power and Civil Society in Pakistan,* ed. Anita Weiss and S. Zulfikar Gilani, 217-47. Karachi, Pakistan: Oxford University Press.

Barthes, Roland. 1972. *Mythologies.* Selected and trans. Annette Lavers. New York: Hill and Wang.

Bassiouni, Cherif. 1987. "A Search for Islamic Criminal Justice: An Emerging Trend in Muslim States." In *The Islamic Impulse,* ed. B. Stowasser, 244-54. Washington, DC: Centre for Contemporary Arab Studies, Georgetown University.

Basu, Amrita. 2000. "Globalization of the Local/Localization of the Global: Mapping Transnational Women's Movements." *Meridians: Feminism, Race, Transnationalism* 1, 1: 68-84.

Baxi, Upendra. 1994. *Inhuman Wrongs and Human Rights: Unconventional Essays.* New Delhi, India: Har-Anand.

Bello, Walden. 2000. "Building an Iron Cage: Breton Woods Institutions, the WTO, and the South." In *Views from the South: The Effects of Globalization and the WTO on Third World Countries,* 54-90. Chicago, IL: Food First Books and the International Forum on Globalization.

Bennet Jones, Owen. 2002. *Pakistan: Eye of the Storm.* New Haven: Yale University Press.

Bhabha, Homi. 1990. "The Other Question: Difference, Discrimination and the Discourse of Colonialism." In *Out There: Marginalization and Contemporary Cultures,* ed. R. Ferguson et al., 71-88. Reprint, Cambridge, MA: MIT Press, 2001.

–. 1994a. "Dissemination: Time, Narrative and the Margins of the Modern Nation." In *Location of Culture,* 139-70. New York: Routledge.

–. 1994b. "Frontline/Borderposts." In *Displacements: Cultural Identities in Question,* ed. A. Bammer, 269-72. Bloomington: Indiana University Press.

Bose, Sugata, and Ayesha Jalal. 1998. *Modern South Asia: History, Culture, Political Economy.* New York: Routledge.

Boyd, Susan, and Karlene Faith. 1999. "Incarceration as a Gendering Strategy." *Canadian Journal of Law and Society* 14, 1: 45-60.

Brah, Avtar. 1996. *Cartographies of Diaspora: Contesting Identities.* London and New York: Routledge.

British Broadcasting Corporation (BBC). 2002. "Musharraf Promises Women Equality," 7 March.

Burki, Shahid Javed. 1984. "Pakistan's Sixth Plan: Helping the Country Climb Out of Poverty." *Asian Survey* 24: 422-42.

–. 2001. "Politics of Power and Its Economic Imperatives: Pakistan, 1947-99." In *Power and Civil Society in Pakistan,* ed. Anita M. Weiss and S. Zulfiqar Gilani, 123-66. Karachi, Pakistan: Oxford University Press.

Cabezas, Amalia Lucia. 1998. "A World of People: Sex Workers in Mexico: Claudia Colimoro interviewed by Amalia Lucia Cabezas." In Kamala Kempadoo and Jo Doezema, eds., *Global Sex Workers: Rights, Resistance and Redefinition,* 197-99. New York: Routledge.

Carroll, Lucy. 1982. "Nizam-I-Islam: Processes and Conflicts in Pakistan's Program of Islamisation with Special Reference to the Position of Women." *Journal of Commonwealth and Comparative Politics* 20: 57-95.

Central Intelligence Agency (CIA). 2001. *CIA World Fact Book.* http://www.cia.gov/cia/publications/factbook.

Chakravarthi, Raghhavan. 1990. *Recolonisation.* Penang: Third World Network.

Chatterjee, Partha. 1987. "The Nationalist Resolution of the Women's Question." In *Recasting Women: Essays in Indian Colonial History,* ed. Kumkum Sangari and Sudesh Vaid, 233-53. New Brunswick, NJ: Rutgers University Press.

Chow, Rey. 1997. *Writing Diaspora: Tactics of Intervention in Contemporary Cultural Studies.* Bloomington, IN: Indiana University Press.

Comack, Elizabeth. 1996. *Women in Trouble: Connecting Women's Law Violations to their History of Abuse.* Halifax: Fernwood.

–. 2000a. "The Prisoning of Women: Meeting Women's Needs." In *Ideal Prison: Critical Essays on Women's Imprisonment in Canada,* ed. Margaret Shaw and Kelly Hannah Moffat, 12-30. Halifax: Fernwood.

–. 2000b. "Women and Crime." In *Criminology: A Canadian Perspective,* 137-75. Toronto: Harcourt.

Commission of Inquiry on the Status of Women (CIW). 1997. *Report,* Islamabad, Pakistan: Commission of Inquiry on the Status of Women.

Cook, Nancy. 2001. "The Discursive Constitution of Pakistani Women: The Articulation of Gender, Nation and Islam." *Atlantis* 25, 2 (Spring/Summer): 31-39.

Corrigan, Phillip, and Derek Seyer. 1985. *The Great Arch.* Oxford, UK: Basil Blackwell.

Dua, Ena, and Alissa Trotz, eds. 2002. "Transnational Pedagogy: Doing Political Work in Women's Studies: An Interview with Chandra Talpade Mohanty." *Atlantis* 26, 2 (Spring/Summer): 66-77.

Dutt, Mallika. 1998. "Reclaiming a Human Rights Culture: Feminism of Difference and Alliance." In *Talking Visions: Multicultural Feminism in a Transnational Age,* ed. Ella Shohat, 225-46. Cambridge: MA: MIT Press.

Dyer, Richard. 1997. *White.* London: Routledge.

"Editorial." 1978. *Dawn Overseas Weekly,* 15 April.

Eickelman, Dale. 1987. "Changing Interpretations of Islamic Movements." In *Islam and the Political Economy of Meaning: Comparative Studies of Muslim Discourse,* ed. William R. Roff, 13-30. London: Croom Helm.

Esposito, John. 1982. *Women in Muslim Family Law.* Syracuse, NY: Syracuse University Press.

–. 1986. "Forward." In *Islamic Reassertion in Pakistan: The Application of Islamic Laws in a Modern State,* ed. Anita M. Weiss, ix-xii. Syracuse, NY: Syracuse University Press.

Ewing, Katherine. 1988. "Ambiguity and *Shari'at*: A Perspective on the Problem of Moral Principles in Tension." In *Shari'at and Ambiguity in South Asian Islam,* ed. Katherine P. Ewing, 1-24. Berkeley, CA: University of California Press.

Faith, Karlene. 1993. *Unruly Women: The Politics of Confinement and Resistance.* Vancouver, BC: Press Gang.

Foucault, Michel. 1978. *History of Sexuality.* Vol. 1. Trans Alan Sheridan. New York: Vintage.

–. 1979. *Discipline and Punish: The Birth of the Prison.* Trans. Alan Sheridan. New York: Vintage.

Fukumura, Yoko, and Martha Matsouka. 2002. "Redefining Security: Okinawa Women's Resistance to U.S. Militarism." In *Women's Activism and Globalization: Linking Local Struggles and Transnational Politics,* ed. Nancy A. Naples and Manisha Desai, 239-63. New York: Routledge.

Fusco, Coco. 1998. "The Other History of Intercultural Performance." In *The Visual Culture Reader,* ed. Nicholas Mirzoeff, 363-71. New York: Routledge.

Gardezi, Fauzia. 1997. "Islam, Feminism, and the Women's Movement in Paksitan: 1981-91." In *Against All Odds: Essays on Women, Religion and Development from India and Pakistan,* ed. Kamla Bhasin, Ritu Menon, and Nighat Said Khan, 51-8. New Delhi, India: Kali for Women.

Gardezi, Hassan. 1983. "The Resurgence of Islam: Islamic Ideology and Encounters with Imperialism." In *Pakistan: The Roots of Dictatorship,* ed. Hasan Gardezi and Jamil Rashid, 353-66. London: Zed Press.

Ghausi, Sabihuddin. 2001. "Police Top 'Dirty Dozen' Chart." *Dawn Overseas Weekly,* 31 May.

Gilroy, Paul. 1987. *There Ain't No Black in the Union Jack.* London: Hutchinson.

Grewal, Inderpal. 1999a. "On the New Global Feminism and the Family of Nations: Dilemmas of Transnational Feminist Practice." In *Talking Visions: Multicultural Feminism in a Transnational Age,* ed. Ella Shohat, 501-30. Cambridge, MA: MIT Press.

–. 1999b. "Women's Rights As Human Rights: Feminist Practices, Global Feminism, and Human Rights Regimes in Transnationality." *Citizenship Studies* 3, 3: 337-54.

–, and C. Kaplan. "Introduction." In *Scattered Hegemonies,* ed. I. Grewal and C. Kaplan, 1-33. Minneapolis, MN: University of Minnesota Press, 1994.

Guidelines to the Immigration Act. 1996. http://www.irb-cisr.gc.ca/en/about/guidelines/women_e.htm.

Gupta, Akhil, and James Ferguson. 1997. "Introduction." In *Anthropological Locations: Boundaries and Grounds of a Field Science,* ed. Akhil Gupta and James Ferguson, 1-46. Berkeley, CA: University of California Press.

Haddad, Yvonne, and John Esposito. 1998. "Introduction." In *Islam, Gender, and Social Change,* ed. Y. Haddad and J. Esposito, ix-xxviii. New York: Oxford University Press.
Hakim, Rehana. 1999. Interview with Rehana Hakim, Editor of the *Herald,* Karachi, Pakistan, December.
Hanif, C.M. 1998. Interview with C.M. Hanif, Principal of Law College, Punjab University, Lahore, Pakistan, December.
Haque, Ziaul. 1983. "Pakistan and Islamic Ideology." In *Pakistan: The Roots of Dictatorship,* ed. Hassan Gardezi and Jamil Rashid, 367-83. London: Zed.
Hasan, Mushirul, ed. 2000. *Inventing Boundaries: Gender, Politics and the Partition of India.* New Delhi: Oxford University Press, 2000.
Hazarika, Sanjoy. 1988. "For Women in India Prison, a 'Grim Picture.'" *New York Times,* 29 February.
Hazoor Baksh v. Federation of Pakistan, PLD, 1981 Federal Shariat Court 145.
Helie-Lucas, Marie-Aimee. 1999. "Women, Nationalism, and Religion in the Algerian Liberation Struggle." In *Rethinking Fanon: The Continuing Dialogue,* ed. Nigel C. Gibson, 171-282. New York: Humanity Books.
Hill Collins, Patricia. 2000. *Black Feminist Thought: Knowledge, Consciousness, and the Politics of Empowerment.* New York and London: Routledge.
hooks, bell. 1984. *Feminist Theory: From Margin to Center.* Boston: South End.
–. 1994. *Teaching to Transgress: Education as the Practice of Freedom.* New York and London, Routledge.
–. 1997. "Sisterhood: Political Solidarity between Women." In *Dangerous Liaisons: Gender, Nation and Postcolonial Perspectives,* ed. A. McClintock, A. Mufti, and E. Shohat, 396-411. Minneapolis, MN: University of Minnesota Press.
Howard, R.E. 1992. "Dignity, Community, and Human Rights." In *Human Rights in a Cross-Cultural Perspective,* ed. A.A. An Na'Im, 81-102. Philadelphia: University of Pennsylvania Press.
Humaira Mahmood v. State, L1, P.L.D. 494, Lahore High Court, Pakistan, 1999.
Human Rights Commission of Pakistan (HRCP). 1997. *State of Human Rights in 1997.* Lahore, Pakistan: Maktaba Jadeed.
Human Rights Watch (HRW). 1991. *Prison Conditions in India.* New York: Human Rights Watch.
–. 1992. *Double Jeopardy: Police Abuse of Women in Pakistan.* New York: Human Rights Watch.
Hussain, Neelam. 1998. Interview with Neelam Hussain, Coordinator at Simorgh, Lahore, Pakistan, December.
Imam, Ayesha. 2003. Public lecture. Toronto.
Ishaq, Khalid. 1999. Interview with Khalid Ishaq, Jurist, Karachi, Pakistan, December.
Jahangir, Asma, and Hina Jilani. 1988. *The Hadood Ordinances: A Divine Sanction.* Lahore, Pakistan: Rhotac Books.
Jalal, Ayesha. 1990. *The State of Martial Rule: The Origins of Pakistan's Political Economy of Defense.* Cambridge, UK: Cambridge University Press.
–. 1991. "The Convenience of Subservience: Women and the State of Pakistan." In *Women, Islam and the State,* ed. Deniz Kandiyoti, 77-114. Philadelphia: Temple University Press.
Jamal, Amina. 2005. "Feminist 'Selves' and Feminism's 'Others': Feminist

Representations of Jamaat-e-Islami Women in Pakistan." *Feminist Review* 81 (November): 52-73.

James, Stanlie. 1998. "Shades of Othering: Reflections on Female Circumcision/ Genital Mutilation." *Signs: Journal of Women in Culture and Society* 23, 4 (Summer): 1031-48.

Jilani, Hina. 1998. Interview with Hina Jilani, Human Rights Activist and Lawyer, Lahore, Pakistan, December.

Jinnah, Mohammad Ali. 1989. "Presidential Address to the Constituent Assembly of Pakistan, August 11, 1947." In *Qaid-i-Azam Mohammad Ali Jinnah: Speeches and Statements, 1947-48*. Karachi, Pakistan: Oxford University Press.

Kabeer, Naila. 1999. *The Power to Choose: Bangladeshi Women and Labour Market Decisions in London and Dhaka*. New York: Verso Press.

Kampani, Gaurav, and Haider Nizamani. 2001. "Pakistan: Shift away from Indo-Centricism?" Monterey Institute of International Studies. http://cns.miis.edu/pubs/other/pakoped.htm.

Kandiyoti, Deniz. 1988. "Bargaining with Patriarchy." *Gender and Society* 2: 274-90.

–. 1991. "Islam and Patriarchy: A Comparative Perspective." In *Women in Middle Eastern History: Shifting Boundaries in Sex and Gender,* ed. Nikkie Keddie and Beth Baron, 33-34. New Haven and London: Yale University Press.

Kempadoo, Kamala. 1998a. "COIN and MODEMU in the Dominican Republic." In *Global Sex Workers: Rights, Resistance and Redefinition*, ed. Kamala Kempadoo and Jo Doezema, 262-66. New York: Routledge.

–. 1998b. "Introduction: Globalizing Sex Workers' Rights." In *Global Sex Workers: Rights, Resistance and Redefinition,* ed. Kamala Kempadoo and Jo Doezema, 1-28. New York: Routledge.

Khan, Ayub. 1997. *Friends Not Masters: A Political Autobiography*. Karachi, Pakistan: Oxford University Press.

Khan, Lala Rukh. 1997. "ImageNation a Visual Text." In *Engendering the Nation-State*, vol. 2, ed. Neelam Hussain, Samiya Mumtaz, and Rubina Saigol, 75-102. Lahore, Pakistan: Simorgh Women's Resource and Publication Center.

–. 2003. Interview with Lala Rukh Khan, Lahore, Pakistan, August.

Khan, Shahnaz. 2000. *Muslim Women: Crafting a North American Identity*. Gainesville: University Press of Florida. Reprinted as *Aversion and Desire: Negotiating Muslim Female Identity in the Diaspora*. Toronto: Women's Press, 2002.

–. 2001a. "Between Here and There: Feminist Solidarity and Afghan Women." *Genders* 33 (Spring): http://www.genders.org/g33/g33_kahn.html.

–. 2001b. "Performing the Native Informant: Doing Ethnography from the Margins." *Canadian Journal of Women and the Law* 13, 2: 266-84.

–. 2003. "*Zina* and the Moral Regulation of Pakistani Women." *Feminist Review* 75: 75-94.

–. 2004. "Locating a Feminist Voice." *Feminist Studies* 30, 3: 660-85.

–. 2005. "Re-configuring Native in the Global Age." *Signs: Journal of Women in Culture and Society* 30, 4: 2017-35.

Kishwar, Madhu. 1990. "Why I Do Not Call Myself a Feminist." *Manushi* 61 (November-December): 2-8.

Kothari, H., and H. Sethi. 1991. "Categories and Interventions." In *Rethinking Human Rights*, ed. S. Kothari and H. Sethi, 20-34. Delhi: Lolkayan Press.

Kramer, Gudrun. 1997. "Islamist Notions of Democracy." In *Political Islam: Essays from the Middle East Report*, ed. Joel Beinin and Joe Stork, 67-85. Berkeley: University of California Press.

Lawrence, Bruce. 1987. "Muslim Fundamentalist Movements: Reflections Toward a New Approach." In *The Islamic Impulse*, ed. Barbara Stowasser, 15-36. Washington, DC: Center for Contemporary Arab Studies.

Levich, Jacob. 2003. "When NGOs Attack: Implications of the Coup in Georgia." *CounterPunch*, 6 December. http://www.counterpunch.org/levich12062003.html.

Lewis, Reina. 1996. *Gendering Orientalism: Race, Femininity and Representation*. New York: Routledge.

McClintock, Anne. 1995. *Imperial Leather: Race, Gender and Sexuality in the Colonial Context*. New York: Routledge.

McCoy, Alfred. 1991. *The Politics of Heroin: CIA Complicity in the Global Drug Trade*. New York: Lawrence Hill Books.

MacKinnon, Catherine. 1989. *Toward a Feminist Theory of the State*. Cambridge, MA: Harvard University Press.

Mahmood, Shaukat, and Nadeem Shaukat. 1994. *Hadood Laws (Muslim Penal Laws)*. 2nd ed. Lahore, Pakistan: Legal Research Center, Noor Villa.

Malik, Amanullah. 1998. Interview with Amanullah Malik, Assistant Professor of Law, Punjab University, Lahore, Pakistan, December.

Malik, Iftikhar H. 1999. *Nationalism and the West: Issues of Identity in Pakistan*. Oxford: Palgrave.

Mallick, Ross. 1998. *Development, Ethnicity and Human Rights in South Asia*. New Delhi, India: Sage.

Mani, Lata. 1990. "Multiple Mediations: Feminist Scholarship in the Age of Multinational Reception." *Feminist Review* 35 (Summer): 35-55.

Mamdani, Mahmood. 2004. *Good Muslim, Bad Muslim: America, the Cold War, and the Roots of Terror*. New York: Pantheon Books.

Mehdi, Rubya. 1997. "The Offence of Rape in the Islamic Law of Pakistan." *Women Living under Muslim Laws*. Dossier 18, BP 23, 34790, Grabels, France, July.

Mendez, Jennifer. 2002. "Creating Alternatives from a Gender Perspective: Transnational Organizing for Maquila Workers' Rights in Central America." In *Women's Activism and Globalization: Linking Local Struggles and Transnational Politics*, ed. Nancy A. Naples and Manisha Desai, 121-41. New York: Routledge.

Mernissi, Fatima. 1992. *Islam and Democracy: Fear of the Modern World*. Trans. Mary Jo Lakeland. New York: Addison-Wesley.

Metcalf, Barbara. 1987. "Islamic Arguments in Contemporary Pakistan." In *Islam and the Political Economy of Meaning: Comparative Studies of Muslim Discourse*, ed. William R. Roff, 131-59. London: Croom Helm.

Miles, Angela. 1996. *Integrative Feminisms: Building Global Visions, 1960s-1990s*. New York: Routledge.

Min-ha, Trinh. 1989. *Woman Native Other*. Bloomington: Indiana University Press.

Mir-Hosseini, Ziba. 1999. *Islam and Gender: The Religious Debate in Contemporary Iran*. Princeton, NJ: Princeton University Press.

–, and Kim Longinotto. 1998. *Divorce Iranian Style*. Film.

Moallem, Minoo. 1999. "Transnationalism, Feminism and Fundamentalism." In *Nationalism, Transnational Feminism and the State*, ed. Caren Kaplan, Norma Alarcon, and Minoo Moallem, 320-48. Durham: Duke University Press.

Mohanty, Chandra. 1991. "Under Western Eyes: Feminist Scholarship and Colonial Discourses." In *Third World Woman and the Politics of Feminism*, ed. C. Mohanty, A. Russo, and L. Torres, 51-80. Bloomington and Indianapolis: Indiana University Press.

–. 2003a. *Feminism without Borders: Decolonizing Theory, Practicing Solidarity*. Durham and London: Duke University Press.

–. 2003b. "'Under Western Eyes' Revisited: Feminist Solidarity through Anticapitalist Struggles." *Signs: Journal of Women in Culture and Society* 28, 2: 499-536.

Morris, Allison. 1987. *Women, Crime and Criminal Justice*. Oxford/New York: Basil Blackwell.

Munoz, Gema Martin. 1999. "Islam and the West: An Intentional Duality." In *Islam Modernism and the West,* ed. G.M. Munoz, 3-24. London: I.B. Tauris.

Murden, Simon W. 2002. *Islam, the Middle East, and the New Global Hegemony*. Boulder, CO: Lynne Rienner.

Naples, Nancy. 2002. "Changing the Terms: Community Activism, Globalization and the Dilemmas of Transnational Feminist Praxis." In *Women's Activism and Globalization: Linking Local Struggles and Transnational Politics,* ed. Nancy Naples and Manisha Desai, 1-14. New York: Routledge.

–, and Manisha Desai, eds. 2002. *Women's Activism and Globalization: Linking Local Struggles and Transnational Politics*. New York: Routledge.

Narayan, Uma. 1997. *Dislocating Cultures: Identities, Traditions, and Third World Feminism*. New York: Routledge.

Nasrin, Taslima. 1994. *Lajja*. Translated from Bengali by Gupta Tutul. New Delhi: Penguin Books.

Nasr, Seyyed Vali Reza. 1994. *The Vanguard of the Islamic Revolution: The Jama'at-i-Islami of Pakistan*. Berkeley and Los Angeles, CA: University of California Press.

The Nation. 2002a. "Hadood Ordinance Turned Out Counter-Productive." 17 May.

–. 2002b. "Some Portions of the Hadood Ordinance May Have Fault." 17 May.

Norton, Augustus Richard. 1999. "The New Media, Civic Pluralism and the Slowly Retreating State." In *New Media in the Muslim World: The Emerging Public Sphere,* ed. Dale F. Eickleman and Jon W. Anderson, 19-28. Bloomington: Indiana University Press.

Parveen, Najma. 1999. Interview with Najma Parveen, Superintendent, Karachi Central Jail, Karachi, Pakistan, December.

Pasha, Mustapha Kamal. 2001. "Savage Capitalism and Civil Society in Pakistan." In *Power and Civil Society in Pakistan,* ed. Anita Weiss and S. Zulfiqar Gilani, 18-45. Karachi, Pakistan: Oxford University Press.

Passaro, Joanne. 1997. "You Can't Take the Subway to the Field: 'Village' Epistemologies in the Global Village." In *Anthropological Locations: Boundaries and Grounds of a Field Science,* ed. Akhil Gupta and James Ferguson, 147-162. Berkeley: University of California Press.

Patai, Daphne. 1991. "U.S. Academics and Third World Women: Is Ethical Research Possible." In *Women's Worlds: The Feminist Practice of Oral History,* ed. Sherna Berger Gluck and Daphne Patai, 137-53. New York: Routledge.

Rashid, Jamil, and Hasan Gardezi. 1983. "Independent Pakistan and Its Political Economy." In *Pakistan: The Roots of Dictatorship,* ed. H. Gardezi and J. Rashid, 4-18. New Delhi, India: Zed.

Rattansi, Ali. 1992. "Changing the Subject? Racism, Culture and Education." In *'Race,' Culture and Difference*, 11-48. London: Sage.
Raza, Ahmad. 2003. "Extra-Marital Sex: A Crime against the State." *One World South Asia*, 18 September.
Razack, Sherene. 1998. "Policing the Borders of Nation: The Imperial Gaze in Gender Prosecution Cases." In *Looking White People in the Eye: Gender, Race and Culture in Courtrooms and Classrooms,* ed. S. Razack. 88-129. Toronto: University of Toronto Press.
Razi, Sabiha. 2001. Interview with Sabiha Razi, President of Women's Aid Trust of the Jamat-i-Islami, Karachi, Pakistan, December.
Reiman, Jeffery. 2001. *The Rich Get Richer and the Poor Get Prison: Ideology, Class and the Criminal Justice System.* Boston: Allan and Bacon.
Rich, Adrienne. 1992. "Compulsory Heterosexuality and Lesbian Existence." In *Signs: Journal of Women in Culture and Society* 5, (reprinted in) *The Lesbian and Gay Studies Reader,* eds. Henry Abelove, Michele Aina Barale, David M. Halperin, 227-54. New York: Routledge, 1993.
Rouse, Shahnaz. 1997. "Gender(ed) Struggles: The State, Religion and Civil Society." In *Against All Odds: Essays on Women, Religion and Development from India and Pakistan,* ed. Kamla Bhasin, Ritu Menon, and Nighat Said Khan, 16-34. New Delhi, India: Kali for Women.
–. 1998. "Sovereignty and Citizenship in Pakistan." In *Appropriating Gender*, ed. Patricia Jeffery and Amrita Basu, 53-70. New York: Routledge.
Rubin, Gayle. 1975. "The Traffic in Women." In *Toward an Anthology of Women,* ed. Rayna Reiter, 157-210. New York: Monthly Review Press.
Sabah, Fatna. 1988. *Woman in the Muslim Unconscious.* Trans. Mary Jo Lakeland. Oxford: Pergamon Press.
Said, Edward, 1978. *Orientalism*. New York: Random House.
–. 1993. *Culture and Imperialism*. Toronto: Random House.
Said Khan, Nighat. 2002. "The Impact of the Global Women's Movement on International Relations: Has It Happened? What Has Happened?" In *Common Ground or Mutual Exclusion,* ed. Marianne Braig and Sonja Wolte, 35-45. London: Zed.
Saigol, Rubina. 1994. "The Shariat Bill and Its Impact on Education and Women." In *Against All Odds: Essays on Women, Religion and Development from India and Pakistan*, ed. Kamla Bhasin, Ritu Menon, and Nighat Said Khan, 82-94. New Delhi, India: Kali for Women.
–. 1997. "Introduction." In *Engendering the Nation-State,* vol. 1, ed. Neelam Hussain, Samiya Mumtaz, and Rubina Saigol, 1-28. Lahore, Pakistan: Simorgh Women's Resource and Publication Centre.
Sangari, Kumkum, and Sudesh Vaid. 1990. "Introduction." In *Recasting Women: Essays in Indian Colonial History*, ed. K. Sangari and S. Vaid, 1-26. New Brunswick, NJ: Rutgers University Press.
Sardar Ali, Shaheen. 2000. *Gender and Human Rights in Islam and International Law: Equal before Allah, Unequal before Man?* The Hague: Kluwer Law International.
Savigliano, Marta. 1995. *Tango and the Political Economy of Passion*. Boulder, CO: Westview Press.
Schild, Veronica. 1999. "Transnational Links in the Making of Latin American Feminisms." In *Émigré Feminism: Transnational Perspectives*, ed. A. Heitlinger, 67-94. Toronto: University of Toronto Press.

Schofield, Victoria. 2000. *Kashmir in Conflict: India, Pakistan and the Unfinished War.* New York: I.B. Tauris.
Scott, Joan. 1992. "Experience." In *Feminists Theorize the Political,* ed. Joan Scott and Judith Butler, 22-40. New York: Routledge.
Shaheed, Farida, and K. Mumtaz. 1987. *Women in Pakistan: Two Steps Forward, One Step Back.* London: Zed.
–. 1997a. Interview with Farida Shaheed, Coordinator of the Shirkat Gah Organization, Lahore, Pakistan, December.
–. 1997b. "Woman, State and Power: The Dynamics of Variation and Convergence across East and West." In *Engendering the Nation-State,* vol. 1, ed. Neelam Hussain, Samiya Mumtaz, and Rubina Saigol, 53-78. Lahore, Pakistan: Simorgh Women's Resource and Publication Centre.
Sher, Ferida. 1996. "Film." In *Re-Inventing Women: Representations of Women in the Media During the Zia Years,* ed. Neelam Hussain et al., 10-16. Lahore, Pakistan: Simorgh Women's Resource and Publication Centre.
Shildrick, Margrit, and Janet Price. 1999. "Introduction." In *Feminist Theory and the Body: A Reader,* ed. Janet Price and Margrit Shildrick, 1-14. New York: Routledge.
Spivak, Gayatri. 1985. "Can the Subaltern Speak? Speculations on Widow Sacrifice." In *Wedge,* 7 and 8 (Winter-Spring): 120-30.
–. 1989. "Who Claims Alterity." In *Remaking History,* ed. Barbara Kruger and Phil Mariani, 269-92. Seattle: Bay Press.
–. 1995. "Acting Bits/Identity Talk." In *Identities,* ed. K.A. Appiah and H.L. Gates, Jr., 147-80. Chicago: University of Chicago Press.
–. 1999. *A Critique of Post-Colonial Reason.* Cambridge, MA: Harvard University Press.
Stiglitz, Joesph E. 2002. *Globalization and Its Discontents.* New York: Norton.
Stoler, Ann Laura. 1996. *Race and the Education of Desire: Foucault's* History of Sexuality *and the Colonial Order of Things.* Durham and London: Duke University Press.
Suleri, Sara. 1987. *Meatless Days.* Chicago: University of Chicago Press.
–. 1995. "Woman Skin Deep: Feminism and the Postcolonial Condition." In *Identities,* ed. K.A. Appiah and H.L. Gates, Jr., 133-46. Chicago: University of Chicago Press.
Talbot, Ian. 1999. *Pakistan: A Modern History.* Lahore, Pakistan: Vanguard Books.
Tandia, Oumar. 1998. "Prostitution in Senegal." In *Global Sex Workers: Rights, Resistance and Redefinition,* ed. Kamala Kempadoo and Jo Doezema, 240-45. New York: Routledge.
Taylor, Charles. 2001. "Two Theories of Modernity." In *Alternative Modernities,* ed. Dilip Parameshwar Gaonkar, 172-96. Durham and London: Duke University Press.
Toor, Sadia. 1997. "The State, Fundamentalism and Civil Society." In *Engendering the Nation-State,* vol. 1, ed. Neelam Hussain, Samiya Mumtaz, and Rubina Saigol, 111-46. Lahore, Pakistan: Simorgh Women's Resource and Publication Centre.
United Nations Development Program (UNDP). 2001. *Statement on Gender in Pakistan.* Islamabad: United Nations Development Program.
United States Department of State (USDS). 2000. "1999 Country Report on Human Rights Practices in Pakistan." Bureau of Democracy, Human Rights and Labor, 25 February. http://www.state.gov/g/drl/rls/hrrpt/1999/441.htm.

–. 2001. "2000 Country Report on Human Rights Practices in Pakistan." Bureau of Democracy, Human Rights and Labor, 23 February. http://www.state.gov/g/drl/rls/hrrpt/2000/sa/710.htm.

Visweswaran, Kamala. 1994. *Fictions of Feminist Ethnography*. Minneapolis, MN: University of Minnesota Press.

Waites, Anita. 1995. "The State and Civil Society in Pakistan." *Contemporary South Asia* 4, 3: 230-246.

Walker, Alice. 1983. *In Search of Our Mothers' Gardens: Womanist Prose*. New York: Harcourt, Brace, Jovanovich.

Weedon, Chris. 1997. *Feminism and the Politics of Difference*. London: Blackwell Press.

Weeks, Jeffery. 1986. *Sexuality*. London: Routledge.

–. 1995. *Invented Moralities: Sexual Values in an Age of Uncertainty*. Cambridge, UK: Polity Press.

Weiner, Myron, and Ali Banuazizi. 1994. "Introduction." In *The Politics of Social Transformation in Afghanistan, Iran, and Pakistan*, ed. Myron Weiner and Ali Banuazizi, 1-34. Syracuse, NY: Syracuse University Press.

Weiss, Anita M. 1986a. "The Historical Debate on Islam and the State in South Asia." In *Islamic Reassertion in Pakistan: The Application of Islamic Laws in a Modern State*, ed. Anita M. Weiss, 1-20. Syracuse, NY: Syracuse University Press.

–. 1986b. "Implications of the Islamization Program for Women." In *Islamic Reassertion in Pakistan: The Application of Islamic Laws in a Modern State*, ed. Anita M. Weiss, 97-114. Syracuse, NY: Syracuse University Press.

–. 1994. "The Consequences of State Policies for Women in Pakistan." In *The Politics of Social Transformation in Afghanistan, Iran, and Pakistan*, ed. Myron Weiner and Ali Banuazizi, 412-44. Syracuse, NY: Syracuse University Press.

–. 2001. "Gendered Power Relations: Perpetuation and Renegotiation." In *Power and Civil Society in Pakistan*, ed. Anita M. Weiss and S. Zulfiqar Gilani, 65-89. Karachi, Pakistan: Oxford University Press.

Yasmin, Rehana. 1998. Interview with Rehana Yasmin, Assistant Superintendent, Kot Lakpat Prison, Lahore, Pakistan, December.

Yegenoglu, Meyda. 1998. *Colonial Fantasies: Towards a Feminist Reading of Orientalism*. Cambridge, UK: Cambridge University Press.

Yuval-Davis, Nira. 1997. *Gender and Nation*. London: Sage.

–, and Pnina Werbner. 1999. "Introduction." In *Women, Citizenship and Difference*, ed. N. Yuval-Davis and P. Werbner, 1-38. London: Zed.

Zaman, Habiba. 1999. "The Taslima Nasrin Controversy and Feminism in Bangladesh: A Geo-Political and Transnational Perspective." *Atlantis* 23, 2 (Spring-Summer): 42-54.

Zia, Afiya. 1994. *Sex Crime in the Islamic Context: Rape, Class and Gender in Pakistan*. Lahore, Pakistan: ASR Publications.

Zia, Shahla. 1997. "Women, Islamization and Justice." In *Against All Odds: Essays on Women, Religion and Development from India and Pakistan*, ed. Kamla Bhasin, Ritu Menon, and Nighat Said Khan, 70-81. New Delhi, India: Kali for Women.

Index